In the Eye of the Wind

FOOTPRINTS SERIES
Jane Errington, Editor

The life stories of individual women and men who were participants in interesting events help nuance larger historical narratives, at times reinforcing those narratives, at other times contradicting them. The Footprints series introduces extraordinary Canadians, past and present, who have led fascinating and important lives at home and throughout the world.

The series includes primarily original manuscripts but may consider the English- language translation of works that have already appeared in another language. The editor of the series welcomes inquiries from authors. If you are in the process of completing a manuscript that you think might fit into the series, please contact her, care of McGill-Queen's University Press,3430 McTavish Street, Montreal, QC H3A 1X9.

Blatant Injustice
The Story of a Jewish Refugee from Nazi Germany Imprisoned in Britain and Canada during World War II
Walter W. Igersheimer
Edited and with a foreword by Ian Darragh

Against the Current
Boris Ragula
Memoirs

Margaret Macdonald
Imperial Daughter
Susan Mann

My Life at the Bar and Beyond
Alex K. Paterson

Red Travellers
Jeanne Corbin and Her Comrades
Andrée Lévesque

The Teeth of Time
Remembering Pierre Elliott Trudeau
Ramsay Cook

The Greater Glory
Thirty-seven Years with the Jesuits
Stephen Casey

Doctor to the North
Thirty Years Treating Heart Disease among the Inuit
John H. Burgess

Dal and Rice
Wendy M. Davis

In the Eye of the Wind
A Travel Memoir of Prewar Japan
Ron Baenninger and Martin Baenninger

In the Eye of the Wind

A Travel Memoir of Prewar Japan

RON BAENNINGER and
MARTIN BAENNINGER

McGill-Queen's University Press
Montreal & Kingston | London | Ithaca

© McGill-Queen's University Press 2009
ISBN 978-0-7735-3497-1

Legal deposit first quarter 2009
Bibliothèque nationale du Québec

Printed in Canada on acid-free paper that is 100% ancient
forest free (100% post-consumer recycled), processed
chlorine free

This book has been published wtih the help of a grant
from the Canada-Japan Foundation. Funding has also
been received from the Literary Arts Institute of the
College of Saint Benedict.

McGill-Queen's University Press acknowledges the
support of the Canada Council for the Arts for our
publishing program. We also acknowledge the financial
support of the Government of Canada through the Book
Publishing Industry Development Program (BPIDP) for
our publishing activities.

Library and Archives Canada Cataloguing in Publication

Baenninger, Ronald
In the eye of the wind : a travel memoir of prewar Japan /
Ron Baenninger and Martin Baenninger.

(Footprints series ; 10)
ISBN 978-0-7735-3497-1

1. Baenninger, Hans. 2. Baenninger, Ethel. 3. Japan
– History – 1926–1945. 4. World War, 1939–1945 –
Japan. 5. Swiss – Japan – Biography. 6. Canadians – Japan
– Biography. I. Baenninger, Martin II. Title. III. Series.

DS890.B34B34 2009   952.03'30922   C2008-907351-7

Set in 10.5/14 Goudy Oldstyle with Geometric 231 and
Futura. Book design/typesetting by Garet Markvoort of
zijn digital

Contents

Preface and Dedication

At the start of the 1930s Japan was not much in the news in the west. Very little was known about the country that the American commodore Matthew Perry had "opened" at Uraga Bay in 1853, and Japan's traditional and ethnically homogeneous population had remained largely sealed off from the rest of the world. Russia and Japan had clashed in the early years of the twentieth century, but after Japan destroyed the Russian Fleet, the Russo-Japanese War was brought to an end with the signing of the Treaty of Portsmouth in 1905, and the Empire of the Rising Sun turned inward once again.

Japan and the Far East in general were involved only indirectly in World War I. Having signed a military agreement with Britain in 1902, largely for naval purposes, Japan was obliged to declare war on Germany when Britain did, in August 1914, after the German invasion of Belgium. From 1914 to 1918 the Imperial Japanese Navy cooperated with Britain and saw some action, but on the whole the Great War proved to be more a game of chess than a boxing match for Japan.

By early 1930 Japan had managed to stay on the sidelines, successfully manoeuvring to avoid the ravages of war suffered by the west. Aware of the degree to which the west had been exhausted by the First World War, Japan took the opportunity to develop its force as an emergent empire on the world stage, asserting itself further beyond its borders in line with increasing pride and a mounting sense of importance. At the same time Japan continued to nurture its cultural and ethnic distinctness and a sense of its innate superiority as a race and a civilization.

Japan had trounced the Chinese Northern Fleet during the Sino-Japanese War, fought mostly about Korea, in 1894–95. After the First World War this powerful near-neighbour was again Japan's greatest irritant, at the core of a complex regional situation. When Japan moved military forces into Manchuria in the · early 1930s to deal with "Chinese bandits," the League of Nations was highly critical of such a flimsy pretext for hostilities. Japan responded by quitting the League of Nations, putting another nail in the coffin of that idealistic organization.

As Japan's geopolitical vision expanded, so did its sense of being slighted by the rest of the world, particularly by the west. Ironically, one of the main sources of this fixation was probably Commodore Perry's forceful opening of Japan to the rest of the world, despite the great benefits that followed. Japan had never devised a way to "save face" after this infringement, and in Tokyo's eyes the ends did not justify the means. Other perceived slights followed throughout the 1930s: exports of petroleum to Nippon were curtailed, Japan's international financial transactions were interfered with and controlled, its expansionary diplomatic initiatives were countered; and, in an excess of self-pity engineered for public consumption, Japan increasingly presented itself as a beleaguered outpost of civilization encircled by the "ABCD Imperialists" (American, British, Chinese, and Dutch). The romantic Samurai warrior had always been an important facet of Japanese culture and the reputation of Japan's military leaders now increased to such an extent that by the mid-1930s they had effectively taken over the country, leading ultimately to Japan's attack on Pearl Harbor on 7 December 1941.

These events were still in the future when Hans Baenninger and Ethel Kyle met in Yokohama and began their courtship. In 1933 they were capable adventurous young people who had both

∧

made the courageous and, in those days, unusual decision to stake out their future in a challenging and exotic place far from their respective homes in Switzerland and Canada, pleasantly unaware of any menacing geopolitical undercurrents. They were not ignorant or disinterested in what was going on around them, but they were focused on their own lives, and life for expatriates in the Far East still followed the same congenial pattern established by Britain in the nineteenth century during the Raj in India. Nobody wanted it to end. They wanted to continue to enjoy the sailing, the cocktail parties, the life of colonial ease, and the reassuring sense of superiority still maintained by expatriate foreigners.

The unpredictability of life in the twenty-first century, the lurking threat of terrorism, the rootlessness of present-day international living bear a resemblance to life in Japan at the beginning of the 1930s. But insular attitudes and blindspots were easier to sustain at a time when it took two weeks to pitch and roll from Japan to Canada on a ship much smaller than an ordinary modern cruiseship; when international telephone service was a rarity; when intercontinental mail took six weeks to arrive at its destination and faxes, e-mail, cash machines, and online tickets had not even been thought of; and when borders of countries could suddenly close with the sharp snap of a bear trap. It was a world of much charm but also great inconvenience and danger.

In the Eye of the Wind is a story about our parents, Hans and Ethel Baenninger, and the first ten years of their life together. It is about a young family vainly trying to duck the onrush of history as they sought a home, a safe home while the world went to war. Sailboats, ocean liners, and steamships were the links of their life in Japan, Switzerland where Dad came from, and Canada where Mum was born and grew up. Indeed, this part of their life story ends in Halifax harbour on Christmas Day 1942 – Mum's thirty-sixth birthday – after their escape from Japan and their brave passage across the North Atlantic where icebergs and German submarines lay in wait.

Most of us view our parents as special and ours certainly did live their loves on a glamorous stage filled with intrigue – and overwhelmingly bad events. Hans and Ethel managed to have a good life together at the very end of the colonial era before the war brought that world crashing down around them. One of us, Ron, joined the story in 1937. Martin, an early baby-boomer, came on the scene at the end of the war in 1945, three days before President Franklin Roosevelt died. It seemed to both of us, as we reached the age of reflection, that it was time to capture some memories of the generation before ours, memories of ordinary people who were desperately trying to live their lives and stay out of the way of the historical forces that dominated the twentieth century.

Memories of individual people who are still living are called oral history. Hans Baenninger was 101 years old when we finished writing this book. The sights and sounds and emotions it recounts still stirred him until his death. But now he is gone, and those *living* memories have disappeared. Transforming living memories into written history is what we have tried to do here. Very few brothers have a chance to piece together a story like this, which is historic but more modern than we think and, we hope, worth reading. We dedicate it to our parents.

Thanks and Acknowledgments

In addition to our own childhood memories, the events we lived, and the stories we were so often told, the principal sources for our parents' story were the written notes and personal memories of Hans Baenninger, who, although gradually failing in short-term memory, retained right up until his death at the age of 101 in November 2006 a remarkably precise recall for the events of seventy years ago that had formed the most exciting period of his long life; and the diaries of Ethel Kyle Baenninger, who faithfully kept a record of each day's activities from shortly after she arrived in Japan in 1931 until her death in 1987. In more ways than one, our story would not have been possible without our parents. We have also had the benefit of photographs dating from the turn of the twentieth century onward. These have held up incredibly well, as have some of the people mentioned in these pages.

We wish to thank our late aunt, Muriel Kyle Kennedy, our mother's younger sister. Before she passed away in 2005, she was able to recount many stories of our parents in their younger days and also shared with us our mother's frequent letters to her during the 1930s and 1940s.

Before she died in 2000, another much-loved aunt, Trudi Jungi Bänninger, widow of our father's brother, provided us with a lot of input about the Swiss side of the story and showed great interest in our project.

Our cousin, the Honourable Mr Justice Larry Kyle, eldest son of our mother's elder brother Alvan and a Queen's Bench judge in the Province of Saskatchewan, provided many interesting insights from his childhood, during which our parents visited Regina regularly from Japan, and also background information about the Kyle family and its history.

Ms Thérèse deRomer, daughter of the Polish ambassador to Japan during our parents' years there and now residing in Montreal, had vivid memories of the voyage on the evacuation ship SS *Kamakura Maru* from Japan to Lourenço Marques in 1942, when she was a teenager, and we appreciate her sharing these with us.

We are also grateful to the Consulate General of Switzerland in Montreal and to the late Mr Peter Hof, consul and cultural attaché until 2004, for steering us in the direction of many invaluable official sources of information about our parents' years in Japan. These included the Embassy of Switzerland in Tokyo, and we especially express our appreciation to Ms Makiko Ohira of their staff, who supplied exhaustive historical information about the development of relations between Switzerland and Japan and the history of the Swiss community there.

We also thank the Embassy of Switzerland in London for pointing us to correspondence between our father and the embassy during World War II, as well as the Swiss Federal Archives in Bern for punctiliously supplying information and copies of all the documents that we requested.

Similarly, the Archives of the International Committee of the Red Cross in Geneva provided useful input about the organization's activities in Japan before and during the war years, about the functioning of prisoner-exchange programs and the supervision of evacuation ships, and about the roles our father played in the Red Cross at various times in his life.

In the Eye of the Wind

CHAPTER ONE

The Meeting – 1933

Hans and Ethel Baenninger first met at the bar of the Yokohama Yacht Club at the end of a relaxed Saturday afternoon, amidst the clinking of cocktail glasses and the happy chatter of yacht owners and their crews. Across the bar Hans saw a new face, a very pretty face, in the circle around Vi Woodbridge. Vi was smoking one of her Black Cat cigarettes and swearing like a trooper about a Japanese fishing boat that had blocked her tack as she rounded a buoy earlier in the afternoon and, as she saw it, kept her from winning.

The new girl was quite tall. She was not dressed in tweeds and a cardigan like most of Vi's chums but was wearing a light, summery frock that was well suited to the warm August weather and outlined her slim figure. Nor did she sound like Vi, who could curse in both Japanese and English with raucous proficiency. The new girl had a happy laugh that carried pleasantly to where Hans was watching; but he could not hear what language she was speaking. Probably English, because Vi did not speak a single one of the many other European languages represented at the Yokohama Yacht Club. Perhaps he would move a bit closer, get introduced and try out his English a little. There were few opportunities to meet attractive single western ladies in Japan in 1933 and he was not going to miss this one.

Hans sailing solo on the *Albis* in 1933, near the naval base at Yokosuka.

There were plenty of Japanese girls around, of course, but they did not really count in his plans. Some of Hans's friends in the foreign community had been unable to wait three years for their six-month home leave. As the other foreigners put it, they had "gone native" and married Japanese. Hans could just imagine what his mother back home in Zurich would say about a Japanese daughter-in-law; not to mention the sharp comments of his older brother and two sisters who still lived at home. Respectable young Swiss men just did not marry Japanese women, even in Japan. In fact, *any* non-Swiss girl would have been a bit suspect to his relatives.

At the moment, she had a crowd around her. He picked up the pleasant, unfamiliar perfume she was wearing, against the background smells of damp wood, cigarette smoke, and salty air. Ah well, perhaps he would have to wait his turn. If she was visiting Vi, she would be around for a while. People did not make quick visits to Japan in 1933 because it took weeks to get there. Unless the new girl came from Shanghai, of course, or one of the other foreign communities in the Far East.

But her attraction was stronger than his discretion. There was just something about her that made him want to talk to her right now. He detached himself from the group of friends who were chuckling at a nimble pun he had just made in English. He moved toward her.

"You never know," he thought to himself, recalling an English idiom he had j t learned, "nothing ventured, nothing gained."

Since arriving in Yokohama from western Canada about a year and a half before, Ethel had seen attractive young men everywhere, but mostly at a distance. Partly that was Vi's doing. She had taken Ethel under her wing and given her a place to live and a circle of friends. Now they were trying out sailing together, and this was Ethel's second visit to the yacht club.

After a pleasant afternoon of sailing, standing around the bar with her friend, nursing a Tom Collins was delightful, and it really didn't matter that many of the men in the bar spoke little English, or none at all.

The trip out to Japan had been Vi's idea. When her schoolmate's letter had come, Ethel was still involved with an eager suitor, but things had changed. Frankly, she was bored with the prairies of Saskatchewan and with her job at Regina College as the director's assistant. And Vi had described the life of foreigners in Japan in such glowing terms. Everyone had servants and lovely little houses on the beach and money to travel around the country by train. Well, all that had proved true enough, and there certainly were a lot of smiling, unattached young men to smile back at, although Vi had not mentioned them.

Ethel had thought she might only stay for a few weeks, but there turned out to be several jobs available at good salaries. She had been lucky back home to land that job as Dr Stapleford's sec-

Ethel sailing with a French friend from the yacht club, Monsieur Humbert, on his boat *Vent Debout*, in 1934.

retary during the Depression. Giving it up had seemed like the height of insanity to many of her friends in Regina. But Standard Oil had offered her a great job in Yokohama and staying on seemed like the right thing, at least for the time being. And she liked being part of this exotic life abroad, with at least ten young men for every eligible woman. Speaking of which – here was that nice-looking man with the strong chin and the kind eyes. He had left his group laughing about something he had just said and was moving in her direction.

"Oh well, let's just see what happens," she said to herself. In any case, her mother had always maintained that a strong chin was a good sign in a man, so perhaps it wasn't too much of a risk.

Hans was a good sailor. Even Vi grudgingly admitted that he was all right. His second meeting with Ethel was also at the boat club, and it was raining. For some reason he seemed to need assistance in looking for a leak in the basement and she seemed to be the only one available to help. So they looked for the leak, and then Hans fixed it – although Ethel never actually saw it – and then they sat on a couch in the basement of the boat club on that rainy afternoon and talked a lot about all kinds of things until it was almost dark outside. He had a strong accent and she loved the way he said her name (É'tel), which until then had always sounded so prosaic and ordinary to her. But he spoke English well, and as a Swiss he knew German, French, and Italian too – he even spoke Japanese. Hardly anybody in the foreign community spoke Japanese, but Hans did; he had taught himself to read Japanese as well and was even learning to write it. He really was an impressive young man, with his athletic physique and his lively hazel eyes.

They found ways to spend more time together. Ethel began to crew on Hans's boat instead of Vi's. His sailboat, *Albis*, was named after a mountain overlooking the city of Zurich, where Hans had been born twenty-eight years before. Hans and Ethel sailed well together and had tremendous fun. They won lots of races on *Albis*

Hans on the porch of his Makado beach house in 1931.

and were awarded beautiful silver cups. As a young, attractive, and outgoing couple they were well liked in the foreign communities of Tokyo and Yokohama. They were superb dancers and glided together perfectly across the dance floor. At parties, in sailing events, and at the bridge table they became an agreeable fixture in the social ebb and flow of the expatriate world.

Other people noticed their growing attachment with a good deal of interest, and they did not hide their approval. At one point, one of the hostesses at the New Grand Hotel could no longer contain her feelings and said to Ethel, "If that young Baenninger should ask you to marry him don't give him time to change his mind. Just say 'yes.'" Hans took a while to get his courage up to proposing, but when he finally did he was unaffected and sincere. Thank goodness her father was thousands of miles away so he did not have to go through *that* agony. Ethel listened to the hostess at the New Grand and accepted Hans's proposal without hesitation. One Saturday morning, they picked out a pretty, unpretentious white-gold diamond-cluster engagement ring at a jeweller's

A yacht club caricature of Hans on the *Albis* in hot pursuit of an exotic fish holding a sailing trophy.

on Benten-dori – it cost three hundred yen (about $150) – and so they became engaged.

Ethel's secretarial job with Standard Oil was an excellent position and she had worked hard to make it that way. Giving it up and forsaking her independence to marry this Swiss was a big decision for her, made harder by not having her family there to advise and support her. Hans, of course, did not have to give up his job, or his name. And he was eager to get married – male messmates were no substitute for a wife. He knew that Ethel was a prize, and that he was the envy of his friends for landing her.

Of course, their families would not be able to attend the wedding. In the 1930s middle-class families did not travel to the other side of the world for a wedding, or for any other reason. The round trip would have taken many weeks by steamship, and the cost was considerable. Hans and Ethel decided to make their first appearance together as a married couple in Canada and then in Switzerland during Hans's next home leave, which was set for the spring of 1934. Otherwise it would be another three years before their

Hans on the *Albis*, gazing toward the NYK Line's *Kamakura Maru*, by means of which the Baenningers were able to leave Japan in 1942.

relatives got to see the wonderful catch each of them had made. So they set the wedding date for 11 May 1934, the day when the SS *Empress of Canada* was next scheduled to sail for Vancouver.

Their engagement was announced in the *Japan Advertiser*, the English-language paper of the foreign community in Tokyo and Yokohama. It was the expatriates' "local rag" and printed all the little bits of personal news about foreign residents. Their plans were also mentioned in the *Regina Leader Post*, but Hans's friends in Switzerland had to rely on word of mouth for the news, as such things were seldom fussed over in Swiss newspapers. Ethel had to give notice at Standard Oil, and her superiors were quite annoyed as they had intended to promote her. She would have become secretary to the president but she decided she would rather be Hans Baenninger's wife.

They were citizens of two different countries getting married in a third country. Nothing was easy; they were both thousands of miles from home, and their homes were thousands of miles from each other. Mr Baenninger and Miss Kyle had to jump through endless bureaucratic hoops and wait in many long queues before they could become "Mr and Mrs."

First, they had to obtain a marriage license from the City of Yokohama. For this, Hans had to appear at City Hall and pay forty-five sen (about twenty cents), in return for which he was given an official receipt that became the basic document of the marriage. There was no ceremony and Ethel did not even have to be present. A city clerk simply stamped the application, filled out the receipt, probably made a note of it somewhere, and that was that – just as if one were obtaining a fishing license.

Next, Hans and Ethel went to the Swiss legation in Tokyo to have the marriage registered legally in Switzerland. They also ordered a Swiss passport for the new Mrs Baenninger. Swiss interests had been officially represented in Japan since 1866, not long after the United States navy first opened the door from the western world. At first they were represented by the Dutch, but the Swiss opened their own legation in 1906. By 1934 their diplomatic interests were looked after by a chargé d'affaires, not yet a minister or an ambassador. There were only two hundred Swiss in Japan so it was a relatively minor post in the Swiss diplomatic service, although it was becoming more important as the political situation evolved. Hans had been sailing several times with Armin Daeniker, the current chargé d'affaires, and knew him quite well.

In 1934 Canada was still a British dominion but had opened her own legation in Japan in 1929 in order to have more control over the issuing of visas, given the heavy Japanese immigration to Canada's West Coast. Consular duties for Canadian citizens in many countries abroad were still handled by British High Commissions (in Commonwealth countries) and embassies, so Hans and Ethel next had to go to the British consulate in Yokohama to register the marriage in the bride's home country.

The British consulate first required a written confirmation from the Swiss legation to the effect that the marriage under Japanese law would be officially recognized in Switzerland. And so it was back to the Swiss legation once more to obtain this confirmation.

The British then considered the marriage "done," and it was duly registered at Somerset House in London and subsequently in Canada. Ethel had to give up her Canadian passport. Ottawa had introduced a booklet-style passport in 1921 and bilingualism became the rule in 1926, not because of Canadian law but because it had been recommended at an international conference in 1920 that all countries adopt bilingual travel documents with one of the languages being French, the lingua franca of diplomacy before World War II. Thus Ethel's Canadian passport, issued in 1931, was in both English and French – and also stated that the holder was a British subject. This practice continued for another fifty years until the Canadian constitution was repatriated by Prime Minister Pierre-Elliot Trudeau and passports began stating that the bearer was a Canadian citizen. In 1931, however, Ethel was no longer officially either British or Canadian but had become instead a full-fledged Swiss.

Hans had to swear an oath at the British consulate that all his statements were true so help him God. In doing so, as is usually the case, he had to raise his right hand and place his left on the Bible. The funny thing, for a methodical Swiss, was to look down at the book on which his left hand rested and discover as he solemnly swore that it was a French dictionary. Seemingly, the consul had no Bible in his desk drawer. Hans teased the consul about his unorthodox oath when they met sometime later at a diplomatic reception. The very proper British diplomat was greatly relieved that Hans had found it amusing and did not make a big thing of it. As so often in his life, Hans's sense of humour had made him another friend.

Ethel had to return to Tokyo to pick up her new passport at the Swiss legation and His Excellency Armin Daeniker, the chargé d'affaires, addressed her on that occasion for the first time as Mrs Baenninger. Ethel, a very proper young lady, said that he ought not to call her Mrs Baenninger until she had been married in church. Daeniker could not resist having a bit of fun with this young and lovely new countrywoman who now fell under his jurisdiction. He told her that he had been authorized by the Swiss Confederation to deliver a passport *only* to Mrs Baenninger, and that was that. Fortunately Ethel relented, so Hans and Ethel became legally married on 2 May 1934, nine days before they were married in a church. They did not even consider the connubial possibilities that had opened up for them in the interval.

The following days were a whirlwind of activity. Not only was there a wedding to prepare for, with all that that entails, without the help of mothers or future in-laws. They also had to pack for a honeymoon that was going to last seven months and take them across three continents and three seasons in very different climates. There were only nine days left, but their friends insisted on giving luncheons, dinners, and cocktail parties on an almost daily basis, some at their homes, and others at the hotels and restaurants that were fashionable among the foreign crowd in Yokohama and Tokyo. Hans's charming and patrician Swiss boss Paul Nipkow and his wife had them to dinner with a crowd from work on 7 May. The following day it was Gwen's for tea followed by cocktails at the Denings'; and then on the ninth it was a linen shower at Mrs Meyer's, with dinner at the Durrers' in the evening. It was all wonderful but overwhelming. And exhausting.

On the eleventh of May Hans and Ethel both awoke early. They had packed all their bags and trunks already, but they still had to make sure everything was transported to the docks and loaded onto the ship for the 2:00 P.M. departure. Then they had to put on their wedding finery and make it to the site of the cer-

Hans and Ethel as a bridal couple, surrounded by (left to right) Harold Schenk, officiating minister, Mrs Warrener, luncheon hostess, Max Pestalozzi, best man, Vi Woodbridge, bridesmaid, and Mr Warrener, luncheon host, who gave the bride away in the absence of Ethel's father.

emony by 11:00 A.M. Mr and Mrs Warrener had invited them to have the wedding in their home, which gave a more intimate and personal touch to the proceedings and helped to make up for the absence of family. The couple both felt very far from home, but their friends rallied around.

Jack Warrener gave the bride away in lieu of Ethel's dad. There had been a lot of kidding around at the rehearsal and when the minister reached the part where he asked, "Who gives this woman?" Jack had finally settled on, "I'm Barnacle Bill the Sailor."

Harold Schenck, a jolly man who was the American pastor of the United Church in Yokohama, performed the traditional Protestant service. (Twenty years later Harold became Hans and Ethel's minister once again when they moved to northern New Jersey.) Vi was Ethel's bridesmaid and Max Pestalozzi served as Hans's best man.

The ceremony was followed by champagne toasts and a delicious lunch, laid on by the Warreners, of cold roast chicken with fresh asparagus, served by white-gloved Japanese waiters. Then most of the wedding party followed the happy couple to the docks in a fleet of taxis to see them off on the *Empress of Canada*. Those on the pier clasped coloured paper streamers that were held at the other end by the bride and groom, who stood at the ship's railing high above. As they moved away from the dock the colourful strips of paper gradually stretched taut and tore, the loose ends falling onto the sea below. Hans and Ethel tossed the remaining bits of paper to the deck, then threw their arms around each other and kissed, to the cheers of their friends below. Their first journey and their life together had begun.

CHAPTER TWO

Mr and Mrs: 1905–1934

The new Mr and Mrs Baenninger were leaving Japan for the first time since they had arrived, seven years before for Hans and three for Ethel. Many thousands of miles of open ocean lay between them and their families. For now, they had a clear sail ahead, and it was just as well they did not know that within a few short years the oceans would bristle with armed menace as the navies of Japan and Germany faced the navies of Britain and America, and their allies.

Hans Bänninger was born in July 1905 in Zurich, the fourth of five children and the youngest boy. He had a happy, mostly rural upbringing in various villages dotted around the Swiss country-side, where his father, Jakob, was the local policeman, usually the only one. Hans's mother, Katharina, had immigrated to Switzerland at the age of fourteen from the Schwäbische Alp region of southern Germany, near Stuttgart. On the eve of World War I Germans viewed Switzerland as a nation whose streets were paved with gold, and the young Miss Stotz considered herself very fortunate to start out in Zurich as a domestic servant and work her way up.

Hans was a bright, good-looking lad who fared well both socially and academically. Possessed of a quick sense of humour, he could make people laugh easily from an early age. He had an amusing manner and a way with words, both in his native Swiss-German and in the other languages he subsequently mastered.

Protected by its mountains, Switzerland was somewhat isolated in the early years of the last century. As a boy Hans could hear the heavy artillery across the border in Germany if he crouched down and put his ear to the ground. His mother used to worry about her relatives back "home" in Germany and took her children to visit whenever she could, usually with food parcels. While there, Hans used to watch the kaiser's dragoons marching off to the front. He was thrilled by the sight of the hussars, sitting erect in colourful splendour as they cantered by, their helmets and lances glittering. Like many Swiss boys he felt envious of their showy brave finery; but he was spared the contrasting sight of those who returned from the front four years later. Switzerland basked in a sort of quarantine created by her neutrality, which enabled her to side-step the chaos that engulfed most European countries during the twentieth century.

Hans used to lie in his bed thinking about the world outside and trying to figure out how things really worked. Often he heard the fading whistle of the Orient Express that passed late each night on the main rail line behind the Bänninger home, on its three-day journey from London to Istanbul. If he got out of bed and went to his window, he could see the long, dark train in the distance, its amber-lit windows twinkling in the night. He wondered about the people inside and where they were going. Perhaps it was the train that first aroused young Hans's curiosity about the world beyond Switzerland. Whatever the cause, he was a small-town boy who wanted passionately to know what lay beyond the confines of his tiny native land. The rest of the family found it all a bit puzzling.

Travel in those days was a luxury that honest village policemen with five children could not afford. Reading, as always, was the poor man's alternative. Hans devoured books, including exotic adventure tales from Africa and the westerns of Karl May. He continued to do well at school and would no doubt have continued on to university in the Switzerland of today. In those days, though, it was mostly the upper classes in Europe that went to university. Besides, Hans did not really think that higher education was necessary for the path he had decided to pursue. He wanted to enter commerce and see the world – the quicker the better. The whistle of the Orient Express was still echoing in his mind; university would only postpone his chance to discover what lay at the other end of the line.

At fifteen Hans entered a commercial apprenticeship after completing his obligatory secondary schooling. An apprenticeship was (and in Switzerland still is) a serious undertaking. Apprentices in commerce spent three years in a structured program, working for token pay in a real commercial enterprise while studying accounting, economic geography, and other relevant subjects at a proper school three times a week. Hans's father had heard of a company called E. Appenzeller and Co. in Zurich that had the reputation of being a sound employer, and through a friend of a friend he approached them to take on his younger son. After meeting Hans, the company agreed to accept him among the small number of apprentices they were starting to train in 1921, and so at age sixteen Hans became a working man.

His employer was in the silk trade. Hans had never really thought about what sort of business he might pursue, but this seemed as good as any, and he began to learn all he could about what turned out to be a fascinating industry. Hans worked hard and performed well. Always on time, he never left things half done and brought a quality and flair to his tasks that went beyond the call of duty. He was soon recognized as a young man who would go places.

As a multilingual country, Switzerland required all pupils in its schools to learn at least one national language other than their own. Most children did not take this requirement very seriously and scraped by with minimum proficiency. Hans was the exception. In addition to his native German, he did well in both French and Italian, and his intense interest in foreign languages was an early sign that he might well diverge from the path chosen by his classmates.

One day, on his lunch hour in Zurich-Enge, he came upon a scene that changed his life. At the time he was simply perplexed by the three young Japanese men (an unusual scene in those days) who were sitting by the horse-trough fountain in the middle of the cobblestoned street. They were admiring the carefully made drinking cup that was chained to the gurgling water spout for passersby to use. The little metal cup was there so that people did not have to share the drinking water with the horses. This seemed to strike the fancy of the exotic visitors, who were chatting in their own language. Hans was enthralled: he had never heard people speaking a language that was so totally foreign to him. He resolved to learn Japanese.

During the third year of his apprenticeship, Hans saw Chinese characters, or *kanji*, for the first time. Like the whistling of the Orient Express and the three Japanese by the fountain, these strange symbols captivated his imagination. One afternoon on his way home from classes, Hans saw a book in a shop window that discussed the characters and included an elementary course of study in the Japanese language. (Japanese uses Chinese characters but within a different structure and with very different pronunciation.) He bought the book on the spot out of his meagre pay.

Hans completed his apprenticeship and graduated to the permanent staff of Appenzeller and Co. In early 1925, the company posted Hans as a junior staff member to its subsidiary in Milan for a couple of years. It was exciting for a young man of twenty to be on his own in a foreign place. His salary was barely above subsistence level, but Hans loved spaghetti and was quite happy to eat it every day – with the poor man's Napoli sauce, made with olive oil, tomatoes, and garlic – at the modest *pensione* where he lived.

One day Hans drove to Milan's central train station with a wealthy friend who was going to Switzerland. It was only after the train had left that Hans realized he was now expected to drive his friend's Morris back to his apartment. He had never driven any kind of motor vehicle and did not have a license, but he was an intrepid young man; having watched other drivers enough to know more or less what to do, he managed – not very smoothly – to get the car back to its parking space in one piece.

Once a month, Hans had to take the train up to Como, about an hour and a half from Milan. The company had silkworm farms there where they produced and gathered the precious fibres that were the basis of the whole industry. Hans was responsible for carrying the company payroll to a town called Campo, near Como, and paying the employees on the farm in cash, a big responsibility for a chap in his early twenties. He gave the employees their pay envelopes as they queued in front of the small table in the court-yard of the farm where he sat. Most of the workers were young Italian women who made suggestive offers to the handsome young man. It was only his profound fear of syphilis that kept him from accepting. Hans always had much to think about on the lonely train ride back to Milan.

In 1927 the company sent Hans to Basel to work with their agent there, a man named Hodel. He was the elderly founder of the firm and took a great liking to Hans, at one point even invit-ing him to become a partner. Things changed abruptly when Mr Hodel's son took over the reins of the little company. Hodel *fils* made it clear that it was now his brother-in-law who was next in line to become a partner, not Hans Bänninger.

In the meantime, Hans had assiduously continued his Japa-nese studies, moving on through other books after the one he had purchased in Zurich three years earlier. When he saw that things were not developing in his favour with the Hodels, he took the initiative. Deciding that it was perhaps now or never, Hans wrote to three Swiss trading companies that had textile operations in Japan, offering his services as a young man well trained in the business, with a respectable knowledge of the Japanese language.

Nabholz and Co. responded immediately and offered Hans employment in their Yokohama office. They proposed what seemed like a munificent salary of 450 yen per month, equivalent to about one thousand Swiss francs. This went a great deal further in Switzerland than in Japan, but it was a good start. Hans signed an initial contract for three years, to be followed by six months' home leave. After saying farewell to friends and family, Hans boarded a train for the south of France on 29 April 1927, three months shy of his twenty-second birthday.

The noise and heat and bustling multiracial humanity of the train station in Marseilles were intoxicating. After a good bouillabaisse and a bit too much wine, Hans spent the night in a tatty hotel by the docks. The next morning he boarded the SS *Hakozaki Maru*, an old and rather unprepossessing Japanese ship that was to be his home for the next forty-two days. He was on his way to the Orient, if not exactly by Express.

Seven years later, as Hans stood at the railing of the *Empress of Canada* embracing his beautiful bride, he felt that life was unfolding as he had dreamed it might.

It was only three years since Ethel had astonished her family in Canada by moving to Japan, but it seemed more like a lifetime. Now she was on her way back to the farm with the young European she had married a few hours earlier to see all the familiar people she had left behind.

Ethel Rebecca Kyle was born during a record-breaking cold spell on Christmas Day in 1906 and was thus about a year and a half younger than her new husband. Her father, Clare Kyle, was of Scottish descent and the first-generation Canadian son of David Kyle, who had come from the Scottish Borders with his wife to help build railroads in Quebec. The family moved to Ontario, near Fergus, where Clare was born, and where he met Minnie Stacey, a proper young lady of Anglo-Irish origin who had been born not long after her parents' arrival in Canada. Clare and Minnie were married very young, and in 1904, a year before Saskatchewan became a province, they migrated west as pioneers, settling on a good plot of land in the prairie town of Richardson, just outside the capital city of Regina, which itself had been founded only a year earlier, in 1903. There they built what eventually became a successful, prosperous wheat farm.

Ethel grew up on the farm with her brothers and sisters. Life was hard, especially in the long months of winter when temperatures dropped as low as fifty-five degrees below zero and the winds swept down across the prairies from the Arctic. It was weather that could kill, but the kids all walked to the one-room schoolhouse, even in winter. The soil in Saskatchewan was deep, dark, and rich, but the growing season was short, and the mud, snow, and dust could turn farming – and living – into a frustrating struggle.

The Kyles were a hard-working, happy, and congenial family. Ethel's parents were both well educated for that era, having completed high school. Clare Kyle was a tall, quiet and very humane man with a wonderful twinkle in his eye and a lean, weathered look that went with being a wheat farmer on the prairies when there was no electricity, and when internal combustion engines were not very dependable. Power meant *horse*power, or *man*power. They all walked together to the little Anglican church in Richardson every Sunday.

Minnie belonged to the Ladies' Aid Society at the church, where the farmers' wives got together to make quilts for the less fortunate and to raise money for the parish. She was witty and high-strung, always demanding the best of her children and those around her. She may have been a farmer's wife in rural Saskatchewan, but Minnie Kyle knew that another world existed. She made sure that her children ate with the right fork, used the subjunctive correctly, and strictly avoided the swearing they sometimes overheard from the hired hands. They dressed properly for church on Sundays – white gloves and a hat for the girls, clean shirt and polished shoes for the boys.

Like the better students in most one-room schools, Ethel was a great help to her teacher, who handled six different grades simultaneously under the same roof. As she passed each grade she would help to teach the younger kids, or at least tell them stories while

Ethel (third from left) with a group of friends outside Regina College in 1924.

the overburdened teacher was busy with another grade. Ethel was a sociable girl and always popular. In the winter evenings, she read by the coal-oil lanterns at home as much as she could. When she reached high school, her parents managed to send her as a boarder to Regina College, where the standards were high. Ethel made many friends at the college, including a few boarders from abroad, one of whom was Vi Woodbridge, who suggested a few years later that Ethel join her in Japan.

After completing her academic studies, Ethel earned a diploma from a secretarial school so that she could support herself. Entering the workforce in 1930 was not an easy thing to do, but when she graduated, Dr Stapleford, the director of Regina College, immediately hired her as his assistant. She could type eighty words a minute, take shorthand dictation, and manage his office in an efficient manner. In the twenty-first century Ethel would have gone to university and had a managerial or executive position, but the world was not quite ready for such things in 1930. In any case, she and her friends did not expect to work for very long before marrying and starting families. An attractive young lady, she was frequently seen driving around Regina, her father's McLaughlin-Buick filled with friends. Ethel was in no hurry to marry. She was enjoying herself and her self-sufficiency and was not sure what she wanted next in life.

What she got next was a big surprise. In 1931 her friend Vi invited Ethel to join her in Japan, where Vi was thoroughly at home as an English expatriate who had grown up there. Vi's invitation was just the sort of lightning bolt Ethel needed. Clare and Minnie had brought up their children to set their sights high and were pleased at this extraordinary demonstration of Ethel's independence and desire to dance to a different drummer. Outwardly they took it in their stride and encouraged their daughter to go if she really wanted to. Inwardly, they were astonished and dismayed, knowing that they would miss her very much. Ethel's teenage sister Muriel was impressed with her glamorous big sister's sense of adventure and bragged about her to her friends at school.

Alvan and Harvey were amazed that their sister wanted to leave home and had to check the family atlas to see just where she was going. Ethel herself was dumbfounded by the way that Vi Woodbridge's casual invitation was transforming the course of her life, which until then had seemed so boringly predictable. Vi's letter, covered with exotic stamps, was a defining moment, an unexpected knock of opportunity that Ethel knew she must answer. She was not unhappy with Regina, but she was eager to see beyond it.

So it was that Ethel boarded a train to Vancouver in the spring of 1931, leaving behind everything familiar and comforting. She did not know a soul on board the ss *Empress of Canada*, although she made plenty of shipboard acquaintances during the two-week passage across the Pacific. In Yokohama, Vi was the only person waving to her as the ship slipped into its pier, and the only friend she had; all her other friends, suitors, and loved ones were now on the other side of the ocean, beyond the Rocky Mountains.

In those days it was more difficult to change your mind about the choices you made. You could not simply decide that you had made a mistake, get on a plane, and be home the next day. At first, Ethel was not sure whether she would stay in Japan. Everything was so different and unfamiliar, and she was very homesick, despite the cheerful tone of the letters she wrote home. Vi was a nice enough girl, but she was rougher around the edges than Ethel had remembered and also rather possessive of her newly arrived friend from Canada. This made it harder to meet new friends, but Ethel was at least on her way to becoming an independent woman. As Vi had rightly foreseen, Ethel rapidly found a very good job, with the Standard Oil Company, in Yokohama. This brought her into contact with a whole new group of people and gave a more dynamic rhythm to her life. It also provided her with a financial base and an expanded sense of herself. Ethel was increasingly happy in her new home and thoughts of returning to Canada began to fade.

She gradually acquired a new social life, especially once she became part of the crowd at the Yokohama Yacht Club. Ethel soon grew accustomed to many of the things that had seemed so strange when she first arrived, although she still did not like Japanese food very much, and driving on the "wrong" side of the road was a trial on those few occasions when she had to use a car. It was not very long before she met Hans, who had travelled even farther than she had to get to Japan.

CHAPTER THREE

The Honeymoon: Part One – 1934

The *Empress of Canada* was the fastest ship in the Canadian Pacific fleet, a beautiful white vessel with three orange funnels. On subsequent crossings to Vancouver, Mr and Mrs Baenninger would take Canadian Pacific boats that travelled without stop. But this time, at the beginning of a honeymoon that was to last seven months, they opted for the more leisurely fortnightly crossing, which made a stopover in Honolulu. As the ship made its way into the open ocean Hans and Ethel began unpacking their things in cabin number four.

Although Swiss companies in the Far East were less formal about vacations than the larger British or Dutch trading firms, an expatriate employee's contract usually called for a period of about three years' work, without any prolonged holiday, followed by a six-month leave "back home." The split, of course, had a lot to do with the lengthy duration and high cost of travel to and fro. The trip home was usually paid for by the major employers, but not always by the smaller ones. Hans had been smart to plan his wedding to coincide with his next home leave so that he could relax. There would be very little demanded of him in terms of work in the months ahead.

This was only fair, since Hans had been deprived of his first six-month home leave. It would normally have occurred in 1930 or, at the latest, 1931, but Hans's first employer in Japan, Nabholz and Co., had gone bankrupt in 1930 at about the time his first home leave came due. Nabholz had been holding a large number of sales contracts based on a price of four dollars per pound for raw silk when the stock market crashed in the United States in October 1929. The price of raw silk dropped to two dollars per pound almost overnight and many American customers simply were unable or refused to honour the contracts, leaving Nabholz with large inventories of high-priced silk that they could not finance.

Nabholz was the only Swiss firm that also exported finished silk textiles, or piece goods, in addition to raw silk. The firm was finally taken over by another Swiss trading group involved in textiles, Sulzer-Rudolph and Co. (which was later reorganized and renamed Charles Rudolph and Co.). They agreed to acquire the piece-goods division of Nabholz, but only on the condition that Hans Baenninger came with it as part of the deal. For Hans, who had suddenly faced unemployment thousands of miles from home because of the bankruptcy, this was a real break and he considered himself very lucky to have held onto a job. But he had to negotiate a new three-year contract with Sulzer-Rudolph, and the new owners wanted to ensure a "seamless transition" in the takeover. Hans therefore had to agree to give up his hard-earned and much-needed home leave as part of the deal, postponing it for another three years. So for Hans the honeymoon was also his first real vacation in almost seven years.

Hans and Ethel arrived in Honolulu after a luxurious week at sea. The *Empress of Canada* docked in late afternoon. They had only twenty-four hours to enjoy this exotic and beautiful island. After looking at some of the sights around Diamond Head they went for dinner and watched the dancing at the Royal Hawaiian Hotel. It was good to be on terra firma again, away from the constant rolling of the ship. They returned very late to the *Empress of Canada* for an all too brief night's sleep and then were up again early the next morning. They discovered to their dismay that in all the rushing around before their wedding, they had forgotten

Office staff, 1933.

to pack bathing suits. Hotels, even luxury hotels, rarely had bou-
tiques then, and so they found themselves unable to take advantage of the glorious weather for a swim off Waikiki Beach. Still
they enjoyed sitting in the warm sun, watching the attractive
golden-skinned natives show off their surfboarding skills. They
had tea at the Moana Hotel, right next to the beach, and were
entertained by a group of grass-skirted Hawaiian girls performing
one of their lovely native dances. Later they took a ride on one of
the charming open-air streetcars. To a couple in love it was all fas-
cinatingly different and new, and they were so lost in each other
that they almost missed the departure of their ship. The crew was
pulling up the gangplank when they arrived at the dock and Hans
had to run and yell and wave so that the *Empress of Canada* would
wait for them.

Life onboard ship was relaxed and pleasant. In the 1930s there
were no distracting faxes, cell phones, e-mails, or tour directors.
Normal life was suspended, its cares and responsibilities banished
for days and weeks at a time. Gourmet meals of several courses

took up much of the day. The rest of it was devoted to pleasure: sunbathing, endless rubbers of bridge, shuffleboard, deck golf, and new friends. There were drinks before lunch, tea in a deckchair with a good novel during the afternoon, aperitifs before dinner, then dancing and champagne parties in the evening. It was an unending round of gaiety and fun, on top of which they had each other. There were movies in the afternoon and they enjoyed seeing Ernst Lubitsch's 1932 romantic comedy *Trouble in Paradise* – perhaps because there was so little trouble to mar their own paradise.

Everyone in the foreign community in the Far East seemed to know everyone else, or to know someone else who knew of them. These connections made for entertaining gossip and storytelling, but they also provided a vital network among people cut off from the security of home. In the Baenningers' case such links paid off in unexpected ways over the years. On that first leg of their honeymoon cruise around the world, for example, a Mr and Mrs Nancollis, fellow members of the Yokohama Yacht Club, were also travelling to North America. Hans and Ethel became closer friends with them on this crossing, playing bridge and staying up into the wee hours together. Nan was the vice-president of Canadian Pacific Shipping Lines in Yokohama. Eight years later, in 1942, he was able to arrange passage for the Baenninger family, in the midst of war, on the final stage of their escape from Japan.

In another five days the *Empress of Canada* docked in Vancouver, where the meeting with the first of Hans's new North American in-laws took place. Aunt Mima and Uncle Reuben Howes were full of wonder and amazement at their little niece from Regina arriving from so far away with this exotic foreign husband. At that time there were relatively few foreigners living in Vancouver and it was a thoroughly "Canadian" city. Much to Mima and Reuben's relief, however, Hans seemed pretty normal – even rather attractive – and his English was good, certainly up to the occasion. Hans and Ethel enjoyed seeing the sights together, although Ethel was stunned by the realization she was no longer a citizen in her native land. Her passport was now the dark green of Switzerland instead of the British Commonwealth blue. It felt very peculiar.

Next day the newlyweds boarded "The Dominion," one of the Canadian Pacific Railroad's crack transcontinental trains that took them through the Rocky Mountains and across part of the prairies to Regina, capital of the Province of Saskatchewan. Two enormous steam locomotives, with wheels taller than Hans, were his first introduction to the scale of North America. The engine's sheer power, as they pulled the train up into the mountains, was awe-inspiring, even to a Swiss accustomed to mountainous terrain and powerful trains. Still, it took nearly five days to make the entire trip from Pacific to Atlantic. The Trans-Canada Highway had not yet been built and commercial airplane travel at the time was neither common nor truly transcontinental. To a man whose native land spanned about two hundred miles from east to west it was overwhelming. The majestic jagged mountain peaks and sparkling lakes were reminiscent of Switzerland, but it was all very unfamiliar to a Swiss lad who had known the names of his native mountains all his life. Then there was the incredible contrast between the Rockies and the prairies, as the couple travelled for a whole day without seeing a hill, just endless flat vistas broken only by the occasional looming grain elevator.

The puzzle for Hans was why one location was selected over another in this vast, featureless expanse. Why build a house or a town here rather than there? Was the choice random? Why was Regina situated where it was rather than thirty miles west or south – or east or north? The city's original name had been "Pile o'bones," from the native Canadian "Waskana," referring to a huge accumulation of buffalo bones. Was that why white settlers had made their homes there? Or was it the railroad; but then why was the railroad where it was?

While Hans contemplated the vastness of his new wife's native land, Ethel could hardly contain her excitement at being back home. The exhilaration of her new life in Japan had not completely erased her homesickness. She had missed her family and friends during this first, three-year separation, and now that she was almost back in Regina she realized with full force just how much.

The whole Kyle family was on the platform at the railroad station in Regina to welcome them home: Ethel's mother and father, her older brother Alvan with his new wife and two small children, her younger siblings Muriel and Harvey, aunts, uncles, and cousins, as well as a bubbling assortment of old friends from Ethel's previous life who could barely contain their curiosity about her new husband. He was certainly handsome, with a nice smile, and he spoke English with a charming accent. Hans felt accepted as part of the family; they obviously liked him and talked to him as easily as if they had known him for years. The consensus was that Ethel had done just fine and that Hans was good company and a fine fellow – a relief all around. The homecoming, complete with a photograph taken at the station and an interview with Hans about his first impressions of Canada, was in the next morning's *Regina Leader Post*. After all, it was not often that a hometown girl could be welcomed back from so far away.

On the Saturday after their arrival, on a sweltering summer evening, Ethel's parents gave a reception attended by nearly a hundred relatives, friends, and neighbours who turned up to welcome the couple and satisfy their curiosity about the groom. Dressed in his best blue suit, Hans was introduced to everyone in the crowd and gamely tried to keep their names and faces straight. He would dearly have loved a nice cool beer or two, but Regina was a pretty dry city in those days and he was out of luck. Ethel's friends were less abstemious than her family, and at the various receptions and dinner parties they went to during Hans's week in Saskatchewan, most of their hosts and hostesses made sure to serve beer, or even occasionally wine – strictly in Hans's honour, of course.

The next day, the family took the newlyweds on a picnic in the lake region of the Qu'Appelle Valley, about forty miles north of Regina. They wanted to do something typical to celebrate the reunion, and since there were hardly any restaurants to go to in the Regina area, a picnic seemed a good idea. Hans was enchanted with the relaxed informality of the people and the spaciousness of the scenery. During the afternoon, a group of North American Indians cantered by on their ponies near the picnic site. Hans had been reading westerns by Karl May since he was a young boy and was thrilled to see real Indians in the flesh.

After a week of festivities, Hans parted from Ethel and his new family in Regina and set off for Switzerland, six thousand miles away. It was an odd decision that neither of them was very happy about, but the couple had discussed it all at length and agreed that it was necessary to proceed in this way. Both of them had been away from home for years, cut off from family and familiar surroundings in a way that no longer occurs today. When Hans first went to Japan in 1927, it had taken six weeks to get there from Switzerland by ship, via Marseilles, Port Saïd, through the Suez Canal, across the Indian Ocean, into the South China Sea, and thence to Shanghai and finally on to Yokohama. When his father died unexpectedly six months after Hans's arrival and eight months after he had left home, there was no thought of returning to Switzerland for the funeral – indeed, Hans received the tele-graphed news of his father's death after the burial had taken place.

Even for a Canadian, it took about fifteen days to cross the Pacific to Vancouver in 1934 and another couple of weeks to return to Japan. It was not something that one did very often, for the trip back and forth by steamship used up a whole month. A letter took the same time as an ocean voyage because it travelled on the same ship. Airmail, like air travel, was not yet common. Telephone calls between continents were a thing of the future even for those who had phones in their homes; and at the time neither the Kyles in Saskatchewan nor the Bänningers in Switzerland possessed one. Sending cables back and forth was about the speediest form of communication in those days. The juxtaposing and juggling of words, phrases, and "STOPs" to ensure that a telegram was com-prehensible but not a word too long became a minor art form; for even a cable of only ten words from Japan to Switzerland cost a lot of money.

So Hans boarded the train in Regina on 3 June for the three-day journey east to Montreal, and from there he travelled south along the Hudson River on the New York Central Railroad to New York City to begin another long sea voyage, this time across the Atlantic. His young bride was booked to follow him, leaving on 23 August for Montreal, where she would take a Canadian Pacific ship to Liverpool. In the meantime, Hans found himself suddenly alone in a strange land. His trip began with solitary sightseeing in Montreal. In Manhattan he stayed for two nights down in the Battery, near the docks, at the Duane Hotel. He dined one night with Mr Wehrlin of the New York office, but it certainly did not make up for the absence of his wife.

Ethel had more distractions than he did, surrounded as she was by relatives, friends, and familiar things. While she rediscovered her prairie roots on the family farm, Hans was on the high seas sailing from New York for Le Havre on the Cunard Line's ss *Aquitania*. The vessel's four tall funnels were reminiscent of the ill-fated *Titanic* and the *Berengaria*, also Cunard ships, and were unmistakable. Hans went by boat-train from the Normandy coast to the Gare du Nord in Paris, then on to Basel and, finally, Zurich. After seven years in Japan Hans had nearly forgotten the beauty of his homeland – the wildflowers dotting the deep green of alpine meadows, the sounds of rushing mountain streams amid fragrant pine forests and cowbells heard across a peaceful valley as the evening shadows lengthened. More than seventy years later, Hans still remembered that "Nothing I had seen since I had left Switzerland could match this jewel of a country; I was proud."

When he left for Japan in 1927 Hans's parents lived in Affoltern-am-Albis. They had a spacious apartment in the district court building, thanks to Jakob Bänninger's position as the local *Wachtmeister*, or policeman. Behind their dwelling was a cottage that served as jail for the occasional prisoners that Jakob captured, and for whom his mother did the cooking. They were usually short-term visitors and not very dangerous. They often helped out by growing vegetables in the garden, and one even painted a pleasant watercolour landscape of the view from the jailhouse window as a gesture of appreciation for *Frau Wachtmeister* Bänninger's cuisine. For many of them their jail time in Affoltern became a happy memory. When Hans's dad died suddenly at Christmas in 1927 at the age of fifty-two, Katharina Stotz-Bänninger had to forsake this idyllic existence and face life alone on a policeman's wife's pension – with typical Swiss logic, this meant half of the amount the Bänningers would have had as a couple. By 1934 she was living in Zurich in a small apartment. At fifty-five she had just managed to escape the advances of a suitor and was happy to have her son at home with her for a while.

Her brother, Hans's Uncle Ludwig, had followed her to Switzerland from their native Germany just before World War I to avoid German military service and had become a successful tailor in Zurich. The suit he made that year as a wedding present for Hans, a beautiful light grey flannel, was a favourite for many years. Hans also went to see his Tante Bertha in Bassersdorf, where she still lived in the house that she and Hans's father had grown up in. As a midwife, she had brought Hans and his brother and three sisters into the world. After each birth, Tante Bertha had run the household while Hans's mother was recovering, so he felt very close to her. The family had originally moved to Bassersdorf from Embrach, a few miles distant, where many people in the village were named either Bänninger or Benninger. In fact, when the family first arrived, the town clerk in Bassersdorf mistakenly entered their name in the town hall register as Bänninger instead of Benninger, since the pronunciation is the same. Rather than make him change it, Hans's good-natured grandfather let it go, and so the family became Bänninger. Outside areas where the German language prevails the umlaut over the letter "a" is a nuisance and Hans had changed it, when he moved to Japan, to the Latin "ae," which is the origin of "ä." (In old German prints the letter "a" has a small "e" over it, which was subsequently transformed into the umlaut.)

Hans was happy surrounded by familiar people and places, but he looked forward to being in Liverpool on 3 September, when he would see his bride again. The industrial cities of the English Midlands, which in the 1930s still brought William Blake's "dark, satanic mills" to mind, were not exactly popular tourist destinations, but Hans's British customers in the silk trade were located there and so there he was too, calling on clients to fill in time before meeting his bride in Liverpool. On his last evening in Manchester before her arrival he went to a movie. After the film he followed the crowd to a large restaurant – a beer hall, really – where everyone sat down to eat tripe with tomato ketchup. Being a devotee of tripe, Hans demolished his eight-inch-square slab of the prized offal with ketchup – and, of course, a beer; after all, this was not Regina. He found it extraordinary to be in such a large eating-place where everyone was enjoying a dish that most people avoid. He went to bed early that night; for next morning he was off to Liverpool to meet Mrs Baenninger, who was arriving on the SS *Duchess of Athol* from Montreal.

Ethel's trip had been eventful and had given her a chance to kick up her heels – to be naughty and frivolous again. She had been one of the select group who dined every evening at the captain's table. For an old seafaring man, having dinner each night with a lovely unaccompanied bride on her honeymoon was a rare treat. There were cocktails at lunch and dinner, champagne every evening, followed by dancing in the salon late into the night. The young aristocratic Sir Ronald S. and an older but very good-looking Dr A. from Edinburgh (who cut an elegant figure in his dress kilt) were prominently mentioned in her diary as dinner companions and dance partners. Every morning she had breakfast in bed, surrounded by fresh flowers, and on the last morning Ethel almost forgot that she had to get off the boat in Liverpool.

Ethel had felt miserable about leaving the warm familiarity of Regina and the companionship of old friends like Margaret Forsythe with her lakefront house at Fort Qu'appelle, and Myra – all the old gang of people she had left behind when she first went to Japan. Why had she ever wanted to get away from them when she so very much enjoyed seeing them again? But after a few weeks at home she knew it was time to leave again. She had become unsure about where "home" really was, about where she belonged now. It was disturbing, and Ethel felt more eager than ever to be reunited with her husband and to get on with building a new home – wherever it might be.

CHAPTER FOUR

The Honeymoon: Part Two — 1934

In Liverpool Hans and Ethel were overjoyed to rediscover each other. It had been a tough separation, and they had now spent more of their married life apart than together. But their reunion convinced them once again that they had each chosen the right person. They immediately set off for a few days in London, where Mr and Mrs McDowall from the British office of Charles Rudolph and Co. took them to the Gaiety Theatre and showed them the sights, including the Underground. They had a smooth Channel crossing on the boat-train from Folkestone to Boulogne-sur-mer and travelled on to Paris, where the company's agent in France, Monsieur Portier, took charge of them. Ethel in particular was entranced by the glamourous city, by the champagne lunches on the Champs-Elysée and cocktails at the Café de la Paix. She and Hans were sad to leave when their host took them to the Gare de l'Est and sent them on their way to Basel and Zurich.

Now it was time for Ethel to come down to earth and face reality in the form of her mother-in-law. Having never met, with no time to get accustomed to each other and no common language except smiles, they carried it off remarkably well. Ethel wisely behaved like a dutiful daughter-in-law and learned as much as she could about Swiss cooking and baking. Her cooking experience until then had consisted largely of helping her mother on the farm and preparing meals for the hired hands at harvest time – plain, wholesome, meat-and-potatoes fare. In Switzerland everything was unfamiliar, including the metric system of measurement. There seemed to be an endless variety of Swiss sausages, and each had its own name: Bratwurst, Bockwurst, Cervelat, Schüblig, Bierwurst, Fleischkäse, Schwartemage, Landjäger, etc. Then there was rösti, the national dish of German-speaking Switzerland, with its dizzying number of variations and twists in the preparation of the basic fried potatoes – with or without onions, with or without bacon, frying the potatoes raw or partially cooked, and so on. It was still meat and potatoes, but so different from home. Many of the vegetables were unknown to Ethel – kohlrabi, fennel, eggplant, an amazing variety of beans – even the pies were different. Then there were noodles, all sorts from Hörnli to ravioli. Having wine or beer with every meal was also new to Ethel. In Regina, the conventions regarding alcohol were clear: people drank alcohol in order to get drunk, and then they did stupid things and had accidents or made fools of themselves. If you did not drink alcohol at all you would not get drunk, and so the churchgoing Kyles drank ice water at meals. The concept of alcohol as a natural accompaniment to food was something she had to learn.

There were innumerable other cultural differences between Saskatchewan and Switzerland, differences that became apparent to the pair now that they were no longer in Japan, a land that was foreign to both of them and to which they both had to adjust. Many of the less significant differences had to do with food. To Ethel it was perfectly normal to serve a salad composed of pear halves encased in green Jell-O, possibly with a marshmallow or two, or the odd shrimp. To a European visiting for the first time, such concoctions were bizarre and to be avoided. To Hans, a salad did not mean aspic but green leaves of some variety with an oil-and-vinegar dressing that had been freshly made with garlic. In Ethel's day, only immigrants like Hungarians, Poles, or Italians consumed garlic, among other myseterious things. In all of Saskatchewan in the 1930s, garlic was scarcely to be found, and that continued until "gourmet aisles" began appearing in the 1980s.

But there were other differences, starting with the physical appearance of the countryside and the resulting sense of place. On the prairies Ethel grew up in limitless space. The ground, carpeted with rich black loam known locally as "gumbo," stretched into the distance as flat as a billiard table and canopied by a huge sky that took up three-quarters of the horizon, like the skies in Dutch landscape paintings of the seventeenth century. The farms themselves were endless: expanses of grain measured not in a few paltry hectares as in Europe but in hundreds of acres. Their occupants, as a result, lived miles from each other. Roads and railroads were the way that people got to other places. Walking, which was the norm in Europe, got you nowhere in Saskatchewan when measured against the miles that had to be covered to visit other people, or go to the store, church, or grain elevator. In the frigid temperatures of winter, moreover, walking could get you killed. The prairie roads were so straight that when they ran north-south they had to have correction jogs every few miles to allow for the earth's curvature, and to keep drivers alert. To Hans it was peaceful and soothing, but also desolate and disorienting.

In tiny Switzerland (a mere 250th the size of Canada), only twenty-five percent of the territory was arable, or even habitable, and what little soil could be found was poor and rocky and for the most part on a slope. Swiss farms were tiny by Canadian standards and the people who tended them often lived in villages nearby and walked or bicycled to their fields. The roads and railroads ran every which way and were seldom straight because they had to go around hills and valleys, streams and mountains. Even the tunnels had curves in them. The corners of fields were generally planted with fruit trees, flowers, or vegetables, to make good use of the few square feet where the crop was not planted because the plough had to follow a curved path. The Swiss did not seem to feel that space could just be abandoned to the weeds, as in Canada. Their sky seemed much lower and there was always something sticking up above the horizon. A few hills stood in the foreground, while snow-covered mountains were an almost universal background. Buildings were everywhere, even in 1934. And of course there were also people everywhere, which Ethel found stressful. She could see the country's picturesque charm, but after the prairies she felt confined and claustrophobic. It made her want to stretch.

In European terms, both Hans and Ethel were solidly bourgeois. Neither of them had been to university, and while this would close few doors to them in Canada, in Switzerland (as in most other European countries) it meant that they would never be the social equals of those who bore the *particule*, the noble "von" or "de," before their last names, or who came from families possessing hereditary wealth. Switzerland was a democratic but stratified society. It was difficult to work your way to the top without going to university, and in most cases wealth or an elite family position – and the confidence and demeanour that accompanied them – were necessary too. Nonetheless, Hans was a smart lad and had in fact been approached on one occasion in his teens by the pastor in the village, who asked if he wanted to go to university. Hans had said no, partly because it had simply never occurred to him, as the son of a village policeman. Besides, as he understood it university was intended for would-be doctors, lawyers, and theologians, certainly not for the "merchant chief" he wanted to become. He wanted to be a successful businessman and, above all, to see the world. He had lingering regrets about not becoming a linguist, studying etymology and ancient languages, but he firmly put that impractical daydream aside.

By working hard at his commercial apprenticeship, Hans had managed to rise about as far as he could in Switzerland without going to university. Being in Japan was like a breath of fresh air for him – and for Ethel, too, though to a lesser extent because of her more egalitarian North American roots. The less-rigid, more relaxed social structure of the foreign community in the Orient put everyone, whatever their social class or degree of wealth at home, on a far more equal footing; for they all shared the basic characteristic of being foreign.

Ethel had benefited from an excellent secondary education followed by a top-level secretarial training, which in those days included Pittman shorthand, business mathematics, dressing well for the office, and learning to type accurately at a speed that would inspire awe in the majority of computer users today. As a single Canadian "career" woman on her own in Japan, Ethel had been outside the social caste system of the Europeans. As a Swiss wife, however, she would have been expected to play a conventional role largely defined by her husband, namely, the *Frau* of a manager in a moderately successful textile company. This would have been difficult for Ethel, who was free-spirited, adventurous, and used to being her own woman, as her move to Japan had so dramatically demonstrated. Ethel had jumped outside the box that Regina represented to her and was now not eager to jump into an even more restrictive Swiss box. In Japan, where they were foreigners, Hans and Ethel could live relatively free of conventional expectations and the strictures of caste and class and enjoy a pleasant and glamorous life unfettered by the labels, expectations, and obligations of their former homes.

Switzerland in 1934 had almost no immigration, so it was homogeneous to an extent that is now difficult to imagine. True, there were four linguistically distinct areas in which people spoke either German, French, Italian, or Romansch, but just about everyone, as well as their parents and grandparents, had been born in Switzerland and had stayed put. As a Canadian, Ethel was more accustomed to immigrants and to a society in which young people often came from different backgrounds and spoke languages other than English at home with their parents and grandparents. But she was not eager to become an immigrant herself in a stratified, settled society like Switzerland, particularly when she did not speak even one of the national languages.

The month or so that Hans and Ethel were in Switzerland was as long as they could manage. Fritz and Elsa Locher, Hans's old friends from Japan, took them all over the country in their new American touring car, and Hans's family did their best with their new Canadian member. Hans and his older brother had been married one day apart (on opposite sides of the globe), but Jacques and his wife Röseli were poor linguists, unaccustomed to people of dissimilar backgrounds, and not much help in bridging the cultural divide. On the other hand, Berti and Margrit, Hans's two sisters (the third, Marti, had died in 1928), were a real resource for Ethel. They made serious efforts to speak English with her and to help their North American sister-in-law to adjust. Otherwise, it was a bit lonely for Ethel in Switzerland; and Hans too felt out of place now that his bride had joined him. Even before her arrival, Hans had discovered at a high-school reunion that it was surprisingly hard to renew old friendships after seven or eight years. He had chosen such a different path that he had more in common with other young Swiss who had been abroad. Both Ethel and Hans seemed to have lost their homes and become wanderers. Ethel, with her English-rose complexion and different clothes, did not look Swiss and was occasionally stared at in the street. And even Hans felt that he now looked different somehow.

On 9 October 1934 the Swiss part of their honeymoon came to an end and the Baenningers were off on their travels again, this time to Naples. Hans had learned that by obtaining tickets in advance to the Fascist Anniversary Exhibition in Rome, they could take the train to Naples for half price, with the other half paid for courtesy of Signor Mussolini and the Italian government. The long train ride was most beautiful, often with snow-capped Alpine chains visible in the distance. In Milan they were met and entertained by Mr Freudwiler, the latest in what seemed to be a worldwide string of hospitable Swiss representatives of Hans's employer. They greatly enjoyed the misty autumn scenery, visiting the Sforza Castle, and eating seasonal white truffles and other delicacies of this northern Italian city.

In Rome, Hans and Ethel both came down with awful colds, but they were still amazed by all the ruins – more than Ethel had ever imagined she would see. For a girl who had grown up in a place that had first been settled in the early 1900s and where twenty-year-old houses were considered old, the age of everything was astounding. They admired the elegant, fashionably dressed people, and Ethel became a convert to European gastronomy. She tasted her first Americano cocktail (a mixture of sweet vermouth, dry vermouth, and Campari) at a chic Roman café and it remained a favourite drink throughout her life.

Two days later, the Baenningers dutifully visited the Fascist exhibition to have their train tickets stamped and found it a bit of a bore, full of nationalistic bombast. They set off for the port of Naples in the south and admired Mount Vesuvius from the balcony in their hotel room. Hans was disappointed by Santa Lucia because it was not as romantic as the song, which he liked to sing while accompanying himself on the accordion. But they were delighted when their cab driver showed them "old Naples" – and then offered to show them "very old Naples" for a few hundred lire more.

In Naples it made them quite nostalgic to see the Japanese flag again for the first time in many months, flying from the SS *Yasukuni Maru*, which was to be their home for three weeks as they travelled from Naples to Shanghai. Their first stop was Port Saïd, where a guide showed them beautiful mosques, steered them through a lively shopping expedition in the chaotic bazaar, and introduced Ethel to the taste of fresh dates. It took a day to get through the Suez Canal, and that evening they watched the sun set across the desert. In the Red Sea Ethel fainted on deck, leading to speculation about maternity. But it was just the extreme heat of the Middle East striking in the aftermath of her Roman cold. Air conditioning in the 1930s still relied on melting ice rather than modern machinery. Hans already knew enough about the Far East to have successfully reserved a "posh" cabin for himself and his bride, POSH being the acronym for "port out, starboard home." Like many such terms used by foreigners in the Far East, it had been coined by the colonial British, who in fact did *not* enjoy being out in the midday sun and preferred the shadier north side of the ship when travelling to and from India during the Raj. In any case, posh or not, the Baenningers found their cabin stifling.

In Ceylon (now Sri Lanka), they visited the attractions of the capital, Colombo, in a rickshaw pulled along briskly by a coolie, then travelled up to Kandy in the highlands to watch the dancers and eat lunch on a terrace bedecked with exotic flowers. The end of the colonial era in the Far East, it must be said, was very pleasant for western visitors. Few of them, before the still-distant age of "political correctness," ever really considered whether it was fair or not that most indigenous Asians could not aspire to the sort of luxuries that were so readily available to the expats. That was simply the way it was.

In Singapore the Baenningers stayed at the Raffles Hotel, a perfect symbol of colonial power and privilege, where they drank Singapore slings under ceiling fans that slowly turned as sweating wallahs (indoor coolies) hauled ceaselessly on rope pulls; they smoked cork-tipped caporal cigarettes, listened to jazz combos, and enjoyed the lavish things that ordinary colonial travellers could do in the mid-1930s. Where such amenities still exist seventy years later, they are affordable only to the wealthy, a great number of whom are now Asians.

Strictly speaking, Hans and Ethel were not tourists. Their travels all had a purpose – going on home leave, returning from leave, escaping to safety – to which pleasure was incidental. The idea of going to an exotic place purely for enjoyment was invented by the British on the shores of Lake Geneva, the Riviera Lémanique, in the nineteenth century, but seventy or eighty years on the concept had still not quite caught on amongst ordinary people. For one thing, travelling was hard work. There were no travel agents to plan everything and there were inconvenient financial arrangements to grapple with. The steamship line or railroad company sold you tickets, hotels would take your reservations, but there was really nobody to put all these arrangements together for you unless you had a company on whose behalf you were travelling.

Then, too, someone had to make certain that locally accept-able currency was available to you in a foreign place where nobody knew you. Travellers' cheques and credit cards did not yet exist and everything was transacted with complicated letters of credit and bank drafts. It also took a long time to get anywhere by ship or train, and only international businessmen, diplomats on assign-ment and people of leisure and means could justify being away from their work for weeks at a time. An around-the-world trip like the Baenningers' honeymoon had to be choreographed well in advance and required careful planning and keen motivation. The enthralling travel memoirs of the nineteenth and twentieth centuries, such as those by Sir Richard F. Burton, Vita Sackville-West, Edith Wharton, or T.E. Lawrence, rarely said anything about mundane travel arrangements. It was only with the advent of Thomas Cook and Sons and their imitators that travel became possible for those who were neither professionals nor rich.

Daunting as it was, there were some compensations to travel in the 1930s. There were far fewer people, whether officials or pas-sengers, to deal with in transit; and since travel was still a special event, other travellers tended to be more polite and well-behaved: there was no "road rage" or "airline passenger rage" in those days. And, of course, there were always porters available to carry your bags and trunks, especially in the Far East. When Hans and Ethel arrived in Hong Kong, they were met and shown around by people they already knew. It was a smaller world, and foreigners, particu-larly expatriates, certainly knew, or knew of, one another.

Now on the home stretch, the Baenningers' ship docked in Shanghai, where Hans was unexpectedly asked by his company to fill in for the absent director, who was not due back from home leave for another six weeks. He accepted immediately and he and Ethel were thus able to spend time in this intriguing city and its surroundings. After obtaining a driver's license from the govern-ment of the French Concession, in which they were staying, they were also able to use the director's car. The roads were clogged with people, bicycles, rickshaws, and trucks, though there were

Hans and Ethel in a relaxed moment on the *Yasukuni Maru* just before arriving in Shanghai, at the end of their honeymoon.

very few private cars. There also seemed to be very few traffic rules. It was hair-raising, but they survived. They were invited through business connections to a three-day Chinese wedding in Wusieh, a binge that began on the train where they were given large tumblers of brandy when they ordered a drink. In Shanghai there were lots of people whom Hans and Ethel had met on their travels, people from Yokohama, Zurich, and even Regina. So they always had plenty of company for sightseeing in Hangchow and the outlying regions, for tea, and for dinner-dances at the Cathay Hotel.

The Chinese had agreed – because they had little choice – to the division of Shanghai into concessions controlled separately by foreign powers, French, British/American, and Japanese. These concessions were like foreign states within China, areas where the laws and judicial systems of France, Britain, and Japan were observed. When he first went to Japan in 1927, Hans had found a large British military presence in China, but by 1934 the French and British armies had gone home and left the Japanese in de facto possession. Their troops were now the only foreign army in Shanghai. They remained for the time being in the Japanese concession, not quite daring to violate or abolish the French and British concessions. Few foreigners in the Far East acknowledged, or even perceived, the spectre of war in 1934; but for those in Shanghai it was harder to avoid because of the polite but grim Japanese troops stationed around them in large numbers, and the thousands of frightened refugees streaming through the city after the Japanese takeover of Manchuria and the rest of China. Ethel and Hans could see that peace was precarious, and they joined the almost frantic whirlwind of parties and nightlife in the foreign concessions. No one had any desire to venture into the Japanese concession, whose many soldiers constituted what amounted to an army of occupation.

It was a curious situation for the Baenningers. Other foreigners were desperately trying to escape the growing Japanese threat by obtaining visas to the United States, Australia, or the Philippines – anywhere that was far removed from Japan and the Japanese troops who were appearing across Asia. Yet Hans and Ethel were headed *towards* Japan. To them Japan was home and they were eager to return after so many months away from their friends and the way of life to which they had become accustomed. They found it hard to think of "home" as enemy territory. Rather, Japan offered a familiar and relatively safe haven from the dangerous and disordered world around them, and a place where their friends were waiting to give welcome-home parties for them. On 14 December 1934, at the end of their seven-month honeymoon odyssey, Hans and Ethel embarked on the final leg of their journey aboard a sparkling new Japanese passenger ship, the SS *Tatsuta Maru*. Five days later they were back in Yokohama.

After staying for a few days at the Bluff Hotel, they chose their first home together, a nice, spacious western-style apartment at 234 Bluff, up on the hill above Yokohama in the neighbourhood where the foreigners lived. They furnished it initially by scrounging around among their friends who were returning home. It was very much like furnishing off-campus lodging at a college today, graduating seniors bequeathing their stuff to the newcomers. Ethel's cook was thrilled to see them back again and returned to work for the new household right away.

The Baenningers' life as a married couple could now begin. And in the pleasure and excitement of that new life they barely noticed that their story was unfolding against an ominous backdrop of increased Japanese military activity and political intrigue.

CHAPTER FIVE

Home in Japan:
Part One — 1935, 1936

One of the great pleasures of travel is the joy of arriving back home. This was particularly true for Ethel and Hans after their long honeymoon. They were happy to be done with packing and unpacking and to find themselves settled again in surroundings that had become familiar. Now there was the novelty of undertaking the routine of married life for the first time. It was a bit like playing house.

Some of the familiar things they had missed less than others. During their seven-month absence they had not experienced a single earthquake, so it was a shock to get back to Japan, where tremors were a frequent occurrence. Earthquakes have always been a source of real terror for the Japanese, especially those who had witnessed the terrible destruction of the last very big earthquake in 1923. But the violent and unpredictable tremors that can happen at any time were no fun for foreigners, either. It was disorienting and simply wrong for the earth suddenly to start moving, and to see clothing on hangers sliding from one end of the garment rail to the other. There was a particularly bad series of shocks just before 2:00 A.M. on New Year's morning, 1935. Ethel had just turned in after a party when the tremors jolted her awake with a terrific start and she reached for her husband lying next to her. The fright was so severe that she felt quite shaky and unwell

– "punk" was the term she used in her diary – for several days thereafter.

Hans and Ethel had become great believers in the notion that every place in the world has some drawbacks. An important secret of successful living abroad is the ability to minimize the bad aspects about wherever you are and build a life around the good things that are always to be found. Aside from the earthquakes, the very hungry mosquitoes, enormous centipedes, the occasional scorpion (which meant you always had to shake out your shoes before putting them on), and one or two other annoyances, they really did enjoy being back in Japan.

Married women seldom worked outside the home at that time unless they had to, and so Ethel became a woman of leisure. She found herself with plenty of time to shop, take German lessons, visit with her girlfriends, walk the dog, bake Swiss specialties that she had learned from Hans's mother, and pass the hours as she pleased. Although she no longer used her secretarial skills professionally, she was able to put them to good use helping out with administrative duties at the International Women's Club and at the boat club. Hans resumed his job in Yokohama and business was surprisingly good, despite the continuing economic recession in Europe and America. Before the wedding, when Hans had lived in Makado, he wasted almost an hour each day riding the streetcar to and from work, but now they were much closer and he could walk. Ethel could pass by the office to say hello during her shopping excursions downtown and every so often they had lunch together.

Hans and Ethel liked their new apartment and were gradually decorating it to their taste. After less than a year, they heard about a house coming up for rent on the Bluff, even closer to Hans's work. It was being vacated by an American couple who, like many Americans, were becoming nervous about the trouble brewing between Japan and China and had decided to go home. Their caution worked to Hans and Ethel's advantage. Although the opportunity came sooner than they would have chosen, they

Looking over Yokohama toward the ocean from the Baenninger home at 66 Yamate-Cho, known as "The Bluff" amongst foreigners.

were thrilled at their good fortune in being able to move into a proper house that had enough room for the family they hoped to have one day. Nineteen-thirty-six thus began in yet another new home.

Before their marriage Hans and Ethel had each rented charming little Japanese houses that they had furnished in western style. Sitting cross-legged on tatami was not something most foreigners were good at, especially when it came to getting up, and they preferred to sit at a table for their meals, which they generally ate with a knife and fork rather than chopsticks. After their marriage, Hans and Ethel lived in western-type houses with partitioned rooms and indoor plumbing. The house on the Bluff sat amidst other similar stucco (or sometimes brick) houses, many half-timbered, with shutters and painted wooden trim. A paved street passed in front. The Erklenzes, who were Nazis, lived on one side, and the Bjergfelts, a pleasant Danish couple, were neighbours on the other. Lawns with flowerbeds and trees surrounded the houses. Down the street, one could just see the steeple of the United Church. As in Saigon, Shanghai, and other colonial cities in the Far East, except for the calls of local peddlers, the exotic smells, and the beautiful tourist-brochure vistas – in Yokohama's case with Fuji-san sometimes in the distance – they might have been ensconced in a suburb of Chicago or London.

The new house had a vestibule and front hallway, with a beautiful hand-carved wooden staircase that curved up to the second floor. On one side was a living room filled with overstuffed chairs and couches, and a fireplace with a mantelpiece holding mementoes from their honeymoon and before. Behind it was the dining room, which was large enough to seat a dozen guests for dinner around the handsome table. Still further behind, down a hallway, was a large kitchen with plenty of counter space, two large sinks, an icebox, and a wood-burning stove. Another short passageway led to the servants' rooms, furnished in the Japanese manner with futon, tatami, and hanging scrolls on the walls, and lit by oil lamps. A cozy library-den containing Hans's desk nestled across from the living room. Upstairs there were two large bedrooms and a bathroom. There was no garage, which did not much matter because they had no car.

Hans and Ethel always had servants in Japan, before and after they were married. It was part of how foreigners lived at the time and was taken for granted. Prior to World War II, the average standard of living for Japanese in Japan was not very high. To better their conditions, substantial numbers of young Japanese left for California if they could (a move many of them came to regret when war broke out), or became servants of foreigners if they were unable to leave Japan. Because the income disparity between poor and rich has always been much smaller in Japan than in the United States or other parts of the West, it was uncommon for

Hans with his close friend and messmate Max Pestalozzi, and a group of
Japanese colleagues by the Inland Sea (about 1933).

even wealthy Japanese to have servants. Most servants seemed to
prefer working for foreigners than for other Japanese anyway, and
so it was easy for "expats" to get household staff at reasonable cost.
Foreigners, it was said, paid better and treated servants with more
kindness and consideration than Japanese employers, who tended
to treat them as inferiors. On New Year's Day, 1936, after Hans
and Ethel had moved to the new house, their old gardener paid
them his traditional New Year's Day visit, all dressed up, and said
that he had come to see them once more to thank them for their

kindness. It was the first time in his life that his employers had treated him like a human being and he wanted to tell them that he would never forget.

Before marrying, Hans and his housemate, Max Pestalozzi, had had a cook who came to them highly recommended by his former employer, a Swiss physician named Rheinhardt who had taught Sugiura everything she knew about Swiss cuisine. Sugiura-san was masterful, a veritable cordon bleu who knew how to prepare all the German-Swiss specialties, most of which involve a great deal of cream, cheese, and fried potatoes: Dr Rheinhardt had obviously not been a cardiologist. Invitations to dine at home with Max and Hans at their small but charming beach house at Makado were eagerly accepted by all the foreigners, especially the Swiss.

When Europeans returned home for good at the end of a posting in Japan, friends remaining behind often vied for the services of their cook, who would usually have been trained (most often by the wife, or "oku-san") to prepare all sorts of dishes, particularly from the employer's homeland. A Japanese cook like Sugiura, who could make Hans's mother's recipe for sauerbraten and dumplings or *geschnetzeltes Kalbsfleisch mit Rösti* in the Zurich style (thinly cut veal in a rich sauce with fried potatoes), would be much sought after. Ethel and Vi also shared a cook at their little house, but nobody fought over their cook when Ethel got married and Vi moved elsewhere. Perhaps this reflected the small number of Canadians in Japan – or the general view of British-Canadian cuisine.

Like most middle-class people who grew up in North America, Ethel was not at ease with servants and was embarrassed about having them living under the same roof, there all the time to do her bidding. Only a few very wealthy people had a live-in maid or cook in Regina, and Ethel knew she was now the envy of all her friends there. One notable exception was a socialist friend from Regina College who berated her in letters for "taking advantage of the downtrodden masses." But Ethel knew perfectly well that was hogwash; the servants competed keenly to get the jobs and she treated them with respect and affection. Paid a decent salary of twelve yen per month on top of room and board, they were certainly not slaves. Employers also had to pay the city an annual tax of ten yen for each servant. Hans was no more used to servants than Ethel was, but he was out of the house much more and tended to take them for granted.

Kiku-san was an older woman who cooked for Hans and Ethel for several years and lived, together with their maid Kiyo-san, in a comfortable apartment connected to the kitchen of the Baenningers' house. Both women worked hard and were devoted to their employers, who considered them members of the household. Kiku-san's husband had been killed in a fishing accident during a typhoon. Kiyo-san, a lovely young woman who was training to be a wife and homemaker, looked forward to the time when she would have acquired the necessary skills and saved enough money to marry her young man. Both Kiku-san and Kiyo-san normally wore kimonos.

From the outset of her marriage, Ethel was never obliged to do things like cook, dust, make beds, sweep, clean windows, or shop for groceries. While she was not much interested in any of these chores, she had been brought up on a prairie farm where wives toiled just as hard as their men, not only preparing meals but also carrying them out to the hands in the fields during harvest time. Sometimes she thought back to her farm life and felt guilty about what she imagined her mother must think. Chances are that her mother thought nothing of it at all, except to envy her daughter's good fortune. Later, when she was left, like most of the world's women, bringing up her family on her own, with the help of a cleaning lady a half-day each week, Ethel realized how lucky she had been. Planning menus was one thing, actually producing them quite another.

Ethel and Kiku-san became accustomed to working contentedly alongside each other in the kitchen, the older woman covering her kimono with a "haori" to keep it clean. Ethel never came close to mastering Japanese, but she could get along, especially with Kiku-san and Kiyo-san, who were so patient with her halting efforts to speak their language and became good at interpreting her nonverbal speech and hand gestures. Hans was always there to handle more important discussions.

Earning their salaries was in most cases relatively pleasant for foreigners in Asia. Their jobs were typically in branches of foreign firms whose head offices were far away in Europe or America. An exchange of letters with headquarters usually took at least six weeks, so the branch office staff were pretty much on their own, obliged to make many decisions that they would normally have been required to refer to higher-ups had head office been closer. Only orders, financial transfers, and other urgent business were dealt with by cablegram.

Like most of the other foreigners, Hans and Ethel continued to spend many of their leisure hours at the Yokohama Yacht Club. The boat club was the centre of social life for most of the foreign community, even those who were not avid sailors, and special dinners, celebrations, dances, bridge games, darts tournaments, sailing regattas, or rowing and swimming competitions were held almost every weekend. The Swiss, probably because of their home-guard militia in which all men aged twenty or more were obliged to serve, were particularly keen on organizing target shooting. Ethel frequently competed in contests with Hans and others and became a fine shot.

There was hiking to suit all levels in the beautiful Japanese countryside, and on several occasions Hans and Ethel climbed Mount Fuji, the pictorial trademark of Japan and the mountain venerated by all Japanese. In summer, there were five different paths to Fuji-san's white-crested summit, each about twenty kilometres up and down again. It took a full twelve hours to go up and back, but Hans and Ethel preferred to do the trip in one day rather than stay overnight in one of the ten well-equipped stone huts along the routes. Ethel enjoyed hiking, and the rural scenery of the tea plantations, the terraced rice paddies tended by straw-hatted peasants, and the occasional wandering farm animal seemed wonderfully foreign, very far from the flat wheat farms in Richardson.

Ethel also walked their dog, a black chow named Blacky, several times a day. She never took up skiing, though, so Hans, who as a bachelor had spent many winter weekends on the slopes in the so-called "Japanese Alps," reluctantly gave it up as well. Skating was another matter, however, and they both happily donned blades during the winter months. Occasionally there were hockey games and it always seemed strange to Ethel to watch her homeland's national game being played in such an unlikely place as Japan. On one occasion, she and Hans had the pleasure of seeing a visiting Canadian team beat the "All Japan" team seventeen to zero at a rink in Tokyo. Afterwards they celebrated the lopsided victory with a bottle of champagne at their favourite bar.

Both Baenningers were keen swimmers and Ethel was especially proud of her championship-calibre backstroke, which made up for her mediocre crawl. Both of them had become expert sailors, and Ethel also liked canoeing, while Hans preferred sculling. Now and then they had the chance to play tennis, though less expertly. When not doing something outdoors, they had ample time to write long letters to their families and friends all over the world. Movies were another favourite (and still relatively new) source of entertainment. There was the Odeon in Yokohama, but the Baenningers preferred an unusual international cinema in Tokyo and often went to it, alone or with friends. The theatre in Tokyo was a kind of Tower of Babel in which up-to-date films from all over the world were shown in their original languages, undubbed. This suited Hans very well. Ethel had to be choosier, but then, as now, a majority of the films were American or British anyway, so language was usually not a problem. The couple generally made the half-hour ride into Tokyo on the electric express train after Hans got off work and arrived in plenty of time for the film. Afterwards, they sometimes had dinner at the Prunier Grill, or more often, at their favourite restaurant, the Mon Ami, famous for its fried oysters. This was essentially a European dish but done in the Japanese way with a light and crispy tempura batter. After the meal, they took the electric train back to Yokohama, or sometimes a taxi if it got too late.

Neither Ethel nor Hans ever developed a taste for Japanese food. It was referred to as "Japanese chow" and they avoided it, like most foreigners except those whose cooks had not learned foreign recipes. Even the well-meaning and dedicated American missionaries rarely had any desire to "go native" by eating the healthy but very different diet of ordinary Japanese. To the British and Americans of that era, a breakfast without bacon and eggs was a pretty poor thing, and for continental Europeans there were bakeries that specialized in the requisite breads and patisseries. Rice, raw fish, and pickled vegetables at the break of day – or at any other time – just did not measure up for most foreigners, although sometimes they had no choice, such as when they were in small country hotels in places like Miyanoshita or Karuizawa, or in the Japanese Alps on skiing vacations. The Japanese had not yet acquired any desire to try western foods either, and it is remarkable to see how dramatically habits have changed in the last seventy years. The sight of young Japanese eating pizza or hamburgers in downtown Yokohama and Tokyo would have been unbelievable in the 1930s, just as the current popularity of the Japanese restaurants and sushi bars all over the world would have astonished foreigners in Japan at the time. In the 1930s people kept their culinary identities distinct. The French ate French food, the Japanese ate Japanese food, and the British ate British food (for better or for worse).

Ethel often went to Hayama for the day, either alone or with friends. Hayama is a small seaside resort easily reached by train throughout the week. It was the favourite resort of the emperor, Hirohito, a noted marine biologist who loved to carry out research along this beautiful coast. Hans and Ethel sometimes went to Hayama together at the weekend.

They especially enjoyed one particular weekend on the distant Izu Peninsula, which jutted out into the Pacific about a hundred miles from Yokohama. Even from that distance, Hans and Ethel could see Fujiyama reflected in the sea-green water of Lake Ashinoko, an enchanting place where their day-to-day life seemed to have been put on hold. The Japanese Government Railway carried them to Shimoda, a small sailing port facing the Pacific. The rustic fishing village was surrounded by deep, silent pine forests. The ocean could be heard murmuring in the distance, like a conch shell held over your ear. The natural hot springs of Shuzenji hissed softly and gave off a slightly sulfurous smell. It promised to be a really lovely weekend.

A gaggle of innkeepers met the train, jostling and haggling with the visitors. Hans secured a room at a fair price – higher than most Japanese would pay, but less than if Hans had not spoken Japanese, or if they had appeared to come from the upper class of foreigners, all dressed up or arriving by private car. Ethel loved the freedom of travelling with almost no luggage except for a camera, Hans's pipe, and some Japanese tobacco. In Canada, couples arriving at hotels without luggage were viewed with suspicion, but in Japan it was expected that the simple country inns, called ryokan, would gladly supply guests with everything they might need, starting with a kimono and sleepwear and extending to a hygienically sealed toothbrush, some rock salt in lieu of toothpaste, and a clean comb.

At the door of their inn, Hans and Ethel exchanged their hiking boots for slippers, provided by the inn, to be worn inside except in their own room, where a second pair of slippers was to be worn, or the bathroom, where yet another pair was supplied. Thank goodness Ethel did not have to hobble around on a pair of "geta," those infernal thonged sandals that were always too small for western feet and very difficult to walk in. Laid out in the room were two kimonos each, an elegant padded open-sleeved outer kimono, or "dotera," bearing the insignia of the inn, and a lighter, plainer inner one. The inn had its own hot water supply, so after a cup of steaming tea they could take a bath, if not privately, at least without having to go to one of the public bathhouses on the main road marked by tall chimneys banded with red.

Even after four years among the otherwise very reserved Japanese, Ethel was not yet used to public baths and she hoped very much that none of the other guests at the inn wanted to bathe in the single facility that the inn provided just when she and Hans did. This had happened before she was married on weekend jaunts with Vi. At the more crowded resorts near Tokyo, when she had had no husband along to frown at the gawkers, there had been several men who were rude enough to stare. Vi was used to that and did not seem to mind at all, but it was not an experience that Ethel wished to repeat. Now, however, she and Hans had the bath facility to themselves. It was traditional for wives to bathe after their husbands in Japan, so Ethel watched while Hans was scrubbed by an attractive young Japanese woman as he sat on a little three-legged stool next to the large tub. Then it was Ethel's turn to be rubbed, after which she joined her husband in the wooden tub. The little stove at the end of the tub sputtered and smoked, and the crackling wood smelled nice. The water was perfect, not as hot as the Japanese liked it but just right for the foreign lady. Ethel heard the characteristic call of a tofu peddler as he passed the inn – "TOH-foo, TOH-foo."

Sure enough there was fried tofu for dinner, with rice and a kind of fish paste, served all at once on separate plates with taro, onion, and pickled radish. Even with the warm sake they drank as accompaniment, it was a pretty scanty repast, but two musicians softly played a samisen and a koto over against one wall, and the little restaurant was lovely. Ethel was always amazed at the Japanese passion for cleanliness – those rush-covered rice-straw tatami on the floor, the general spotlessness, even the chopsticks that you had to split apart, which guaranteed that nobody had used them before you. In some towns on the Saskatchewan prairies the coolies who had built the transcontinental railroad had left behind a

Chinese restaurant – often they were the *only* restaurants – where the chopsticks had always looked well used. But you certainly got more food on your plate in Canada, probably because the Chinese who founded those restaurants had honed their appetites with hard physical work. Another odd thing in Japan was the way breakfast comprised most of the same ingredients as dinner – rice with carrots, potato, burdock, some tofu with dried fish powder, seaweed, and pickled radish. At the inn Ethel would happily have eaten breakfast with her dinner; maybe then she would no longer have been hungry.

After dinner she and Hans took a walk through the village, dressed in their kimonos from the inn. There was a lovely public garden nearby, and private walled gardens on the way. Japanese gardens were marvellous, a kind of idealized nature in miniature, with paths that meandered through a studied symmetry that was very peaceful and pleasing to the eye and reminded one of Japanese flower arrangements, which also seemed to elude symmetry. These were not just gardens with beds of beautiful flowers but microcosms, whole landscapes with rocks and sand, plants and pools of water. When they returned to the inn, the maid had already unrolled their futons and put on clean sheets, and they fell asleep together listening to sleepy birds and lovesick frogs.

On Sunday morning, they were awakened early by the sound of a street vendor calling "Nat-to, nat-to, nat-to." This was a new one to both of them. They decided to try whatever it was with their morning cup of tea and Hans shouted their order to the vendor from the window. It turned out to be fermented soybeans in straw packages, ready to eat with mustard and soy sauce. Thank goodness Hans was able to translate so they knew what it was and what to do with it. It was not very appetizing to look at, but at only five sen the price was right and it turned out to be better than expected. Still, Ethel yearned for the wonderfully frothy omelets that Kiku-san made for them at home in Yokohama. Nonetheless, they were sorry to return home after an idyllic weekend and both were a little downcast on the way back.

When Hans went to work in the morning he wore a well-cut linen tropical suit with a silk tie. By then most Japanese businessmen also dressed in suits and ties if they worked in city offices. In country villages, on the other hand, no one wore western-style clothes in the 1930s; Japanese men usually wore a *yukata*, a plain cotton kimono, while women wore a kimono with a long sash, or obi, around the waist. Transition to western dress was already underway, though, and Ethel had mixed feelings about it. The Japanese style was attractive and distinctive, albeit impractical in offices, dirty industrial areas, and other modern settings. It was remarked that women who wore western-style clothes (women whom Japanese newspapers called "modern") seemed to behave differently. They appeared to be less shy and graceful, less diffident, and more likely to talk or laugh loudly. Older Japanese regretted the changes profoundly, as older people often do.

For most foreigners living in Japan for business reasons, the western style prevailed. Japan and its ways really provided no more than a picturesque backdrop for everyday lives that might otherwise have been led in New York or in Amsterdam. The expatriates' homes and gardens, their furnishings and clothing, while often made in Japan by Japanese artisans, were all strictly western. Few foreigners wanted tatami (woven rush mats) on their floors or *shoji* (decorated rice-paper screens) dividing their rooms. Even American missionaries, who might have been expected to adopt more Japanese ways, usually kept their distance from local customs.

A couple of American missionaries who worked at the Ferris Seminary School in Yokohama used to greet Hans as he walked to work every day. Usually, however, there was no interaction beyond such superficial contact and the missionaries never showed any desire to join the boat club or mingle with other foreigners. There were exceptions. Father Kehl was an American priest who had been in Japan since 1882, and Hans came to know him in 1928. After forty-five years in the Orient, the elderly priest enjoyed the company of young Europeans and would frequently join Hans and his Swiss friends for a beer or two. Missionaries in the Far East rarely made plans to go home again; Japan became home to people like Father Kehl, which meant they went into a kind of limbo between two worlds. They had not fully adopted their country of residence, nor had they renounced their country of birth, and so they were neither Japanese nor their nationality of origin. The business crowd used to chuckle unkindly about the missionaries, using the made-up adjective "mishy" to describe their sometimes self-righteous and otherworldly ways. Because of their public eagerness and private unwillingness to adopt Japanese ways, the missionary groups were seen as hypocritical. There was always much merriment during extremely hot summer weather when they took sudden leave of their religious duties and headed up to the cooling hills of resorts like Karuizawa and Negashi – along with all the business people, of course.

Foreigners who could afford to have a motorcycle or a car preferred to bring a Royal Enfield or a Harley-Davidson, or an Austin or Ford to Japan with them. The Japanese car industry was still in its infancy and there were endless jokes about its products. The tippy little Datsuns, which were inferior copies of the very popular British Austin 7, were scoffed at even by the Japanese. While he was single, Hans owned a Swiss motorcycle (an elderly Motosacoche) and later bought a rakish but well-used two-seater French sports car, a Salmson, for six hundred yen, or about three hundred dollars. Hans bought the car from his friend Kengelbacher, who was returning to Switzerland. Mr Kengelbacher had tried to set up a business to import Salmson cars from France and Saurer trucks from Switzerland into Japan, but importing new foreign vehicles was discouraged, as it is today, by byzantine regulations and hopelessly high Japanese import duties, and his project failed. The Salmson Hans purchased, a model from the 1920s, was not equipped with a synchromesh gearbox or a differential, so double-clutching was required at each gear change and the car had a tendency to tip. When he got married Hans bequeathed his Salmson to his former housemate, Max Pestalozzi.

Hans and Ethel did not really miss a car. They took taxis for local trips and journeyed to resorts and vacation spots by train. For short distances, taxis were cheaper, quicker, and safer than owning a car and occasionally became cheaper still when the price wars broke out among taxi operators. During one such price war, it was possible to travel the busy, slow, built-up, and unattractive stretch from Yokohama to Tokyo by taxi (a distance of about twenty miles before the cities converged into each other) for the equivalent of about a nickel. Rickshaws pulled by perspiring coolies were also still an option in the progressive Japan of the 1930s, although they were less common than in China. The Japanese prided themselves on their modern ways and frowned upon the practice of people pulling other people through the city streets like beasts of burden.

Hans's Salmson provided an example of just how difficult Japanese officialdom could be for foreigners to deal with – not yet on military grounds but simply because of bureaucratic restrictions and regulations imposed by an increasingly authoritarian Japanese government. The car was bright red when Kengelbacher sold it to Hans, but soon afterward the Imperial Japanese authorities decreed that, henceforth, only the emperor could possess red vehicles. So all private cars that were red had to be painted some other colour. Hans followed the decree without a fuss, as a Japanese would, and his car ended up a sort of muddy yellow-green.

When Hans went to the office, he entered a world that most people did not know anything about, a world of commerce centring on an exotic commodity whose source had been kept secret from most of the world by the Chinese for four thousand years. For nearly half that time the Chinese had even managed to keep their secret from the Japanese.

Silk, shimmering and sleekly gorgeous, was spun by the lowly silkworm. The Chinese had discovered how to unwrap the fibres from the worms and create what seemed like a gift from the gods.

Eventually, Europeans (the *geijin*) like Marco Polo brought silk from the Far East along the ancient Silk Road in caravans also laden with jade and spices that were bound for the Middle East. For centuries caravans left China for Europe, passing through the parched desert wastes of Central Asia, via Samarkand and Baghdad to ports like Antioch and Alexandria. There, the camels were unloaded and their cargoes of silk shipped by sea to the emperors of Rome and the wealthy traders of Venice, who could afford the costly material.

When Hans went to Japan, the empress still fed silkworms every spring in an ancient ceremony on the imperial palace grounds. The worms' ancestors had been smuggled in from China around AD 300. By the time of the Showa era in the late 1920s, Japan had become the largest manufacturer of silk in the world, and also the biggest customer for finished silk of superior quality and consistency. Until the Second World War, raw silk exported from Yokohama was carried across the United States by the "Silk Train," which started its voyage at the entry port of San Francisco. The train travelled nonstop with its precious cargo to Paterson, New Jersey, where the American silk mills were concentrated. In the adjoining county was Union City, New Jersey, across the Hudson River from New York City, where a number of Swiss firms created high-grade silk embroidery – completing the circuit that had begun with Hans's export firm in Japan.

Hans had become a recognized silk expert. From the day in Zurich when he first entered the business at age fifteen, he had been fascinated by the whole process of producing silk, beginning with the silkworms that spun and cocooned the fibres around themselves. All over Japan, mulberry leaves for the silkworms (*Bombyx mori*) were carefully tended so that billions of the ravenous little creatures could eat continuously. People uninitiated in the silk trade are not accustomed to hearing large warehouses full of munching insect pupae, but the sound always seemed pleasant and dramatic to Hans in a rustling, exotic kind of way. When he visited the mills of his suppliers, he knew what to look for.

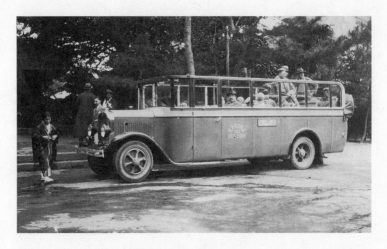

Hans (standing in the back of the bus wearing a hat) on an office outing to Hakone in 1935.

He watched the pupae being killed with steam inside the shrouds they had woven. Each cocoon was then pierced to free the long threads that were collected patiently by hand into skeins. The skeins were wound onto reels in the mills to form bundles of raw silk. Each bundle was then traditionally packed into a bag woven of rice straw; the whole thing weighed about sixty pounds.

Broken or damaged strands produced lower grade silk, and infections among the pupae were a constant threat. Wild silkworms were sometimes used by the unscrupulous, because all over the world there was a sellers' market for the expensive material. In that long-ago time before nylon and other synthetic fibres, nothing compared to silk for sheer stockings and intimate apparel, or for the costliest raiment for men and women. It had other uses too: silk was essential for parachutes, gun casings, and other instruments of war that were becoming more and more important. During World War II, the civilian population in Japan, growing desperate for food, tore up millions of mulberry plants so they could grow crops for people rather than silkworms. It destroyed the Japanese silk industry, which took years to rebuild.

Before the war, Hans's firm exported raw silk and woven piece goods all over the world. He was the young man in charge of supplying silk for the prestigious couturiers of the Faubourg St Honoré in Paris, the gentlemen's necktie and foulard makers of Jermyn Street in London, the mills of Lyon and Paterson, and the embroiderers of Basel and Union City. In the United States, growing silkworms in quantity never really developed, but there was competition from silk industries in China, India, and Korea. In Italy, as Hans had seen near Como, they wove a fine yellowish product of very high quality, but in relatively small amounts.

For most Japanese, traditional garb was still the norm in the 1930s. Silken kimonos and obis added a hint of luxury to lives that otherwise had few frills, and Japan used a great deal of the noble material. Starting in the late nineteenth century, during the latter part of the Meiji era, three Swiss companies (Sieber-Hegner, Sulzer-Rudolph, and Nabholz and Co.) set up branches in Japan and began to export silk on behalf of the Japanese, who were still new to European business practices. As the export business grew, Japanese firms like Mitsui, Mitsubishi, and Equitable Silk Co. began to move in rapidly and the Swiss had trouble maintaining their edge.

It was during this period, at the beginning of the Showa era, that Nabholz and Co. had sent Hans to Japan. As mentioned earlier, when Charles Rudolph and Co. bought out Nabholz (after the firm went bankrupt at the beginning of the 1930s), they specified that Hans Baenninger was to take over the piece goods side of their business, because they knew that the Japanese mills and brokers also trusted and respected him. This was certainly in part because Japanese brokers could speak with him directly, without an interpreter, something that was rare in their dealings with foreign businessmen. Moreover, social rules are carefully worked out and structured in Japan; foreigners who ignored them were simply written off as clods and treated with a kind of careful but distant politeness similar to the way many people treat the mentally ill. Hans, though, knew all the social rules and the proper way to behave as a silk buyer. For example, he would make a formal call on the mayor of Yokohama each New Year's Day dressed in a black suit with a top hat. He gave and received appropriate gifts in the course of these elaborate and dignified rituals – but he could also rub shoulders with the employees at his office in less formal circumstances, or occasionally when the workday was over.

Usually after work Japanese and foreigners went their separate ways. They lived apart, and their customs and amusements were different. Before Roni's arrival at the end of 1937, Hans and Ethel could do any of the things that young people enjoy after work in any cosmopolitan city. They would stop in for drinks or dinner with friends in Yokohama at the New Grand Hotel, or go to the Hamburg Bar for pigs' knuckles with sauerkraut and a pitcher of beer, or drop by the boat club for a sail, a rubber of bridge or a hand of poker, and to see their friends and catch up on the latest news and gossip. Hans would sometimes take his accordion along when there was a party or a dance at someone's house, and on Thursday nights he usually played Jass with a bunch of Swiss friends, a card game that Ethel was less keen on.

The Kiyo Hotel was well known for its "taxi-dancers," attractive young girls who danced with young men for a modest sum. Some of them might have done more than dance; but they were not prostitutes, and further services were not necessarily expected. Taxi-dancers were not like geishas, those formal companions with carefully honed ritual skills in art and music who appealed to the more traditional Japanese. Taxi-dancers were naughty, a Japanese equivalent of American "B-girls," young women hired by taverns to increase the sales of liquor to the male clients. Hans and Ethel were surprised when Hans's big boss from Switzerland, Mr von Schulthess, visited Japan with his wife and insisted on being taken to the Kiyo Hotel because they had heard of the dancers. The Baenningers, with a certain amount of embarrassment, obliged – and everyone ended up thoroughly enjoying the evening

Women who practised the "oldest profession" were certainly present in Japan. They could be found in the "red light districts" like Yoshiwara. Hans was astonished, during his early days as a bachelor in 1928, to see a large banner that read "Welcome United States Navy" flying in Yoshiwara whenever an American naval vessel was in port. Like many other young men of that era, Hans was terrified of syphilis and avoided prostitutes, who were likelier than most to transmit the disease. He thought the American sailors must be crazy to visit Yoshiwara – or else that they knew something that he did not. He and most of his friends were resolved to wait for "nice" girls to come their way.

Some foreign couples got married and started families in Japan, but these became fewer as signs of political trouble began to appear. Like their British counterparts in India and elsewhere, many American women went home to have their children. Very few wives had jobs in those days, so the children of the foreign community were fortunate to have mothers with time to read to them, take them along when they went places, and coddle them. And, with servants at home, reliable babysitters were always available. If they could manage it, most foreign couples went home when their children reached school age. There were missionary schools in Japan that foreign children could attend, but for various reasons many parents were reluctant to send their children to them, and Japanese schools were simply out of the question. There was the language barrier, but there was also concern that their children might receive political or religious indoctrination, or be exposed to propaganda from Japanese teachers.

Ethel and Hans had always taken it for granted that they would have children, and since Hans was almost twenty-nine and Ethel twenty-seven when they married, they did not want to wait too long. Nature was not quite of the same mind, however, and Ethel was very slow to become pregnant. In 1936, after almost two years, she succeeded. But in mid-year Ethel suffered the first of several miscarriages she was to have during her lifetime. Despite her happy marriage, she was highly strung and tense. She may also have had doubts about bringing her first child into the world in a place that, even after five years, still seemed in many ways strange and very far from home, and where political tensions were intensifying. Her doctor suggested that she was simply a bit on the delicate side and urged her to go on trying, something Hans and Ethel were pleased to do.

And so the day-to-day routine of their lives continued. The world around them was changing – and not for the better. In many ways, their existence in Japan was a hermetic one, and they remained blissfully ignorant of much that was happening in the world at large and even in Japan itself. Foreign newspapers were very hard to come by and always out of date. The Japanese press was already heavily censored and presented only biased and unreliable news. Still there was lots of worried talk about Japan's takeover of Manchuria and rumours about brutal events in China. From friends returning after home leave in Europe, there were troubling stories about the brown-shirted Nazis in Germany and their treatment of Jews, Poles, and non-"Aryans." In Japan there were more soldiers on the streets and the occasional air-raid drill. The Japanese people were told continually about the "ABCD encirclement" (by Americans, British, Chinese, and the Dutch) that was thwarting Japan's plans for expanding their "Greater East Asia Co-Prosperity Sphere." This "sphere" was an invention of the Japanese political and military leaders. It was an attempt to give the illusion of some unity among the Asian countries that Japan was adding to those it controlled or had invaded.

But life was still pleasant enough in 1936 and the gathering political storm was not really visible unless one looked for it. Television, with its capacity to bring the world's troubles into one's living room, did not yet exist. Radios and gramophones could provide low-fidelity music, but people did not depend on their radios for news. The BBC was not transmitted to them and there was no Voice of America. English-language newspapers were the main source of news for Hans and Ethel. Radio in English was available, but people were most likely to trust personal contacts. By and large, communications technology still left the population in peace, unless there was a crisis. People did a lot of reading and sailing; they went to movies, collected stamps, or danced to live music. Sometimes they were content just to think. People passed the time by dropping in on each other, writing invitations and thank-you notes to people just down the street, and long letters to family and friends further afield. Hans and Ethel and their circle took walks, served tea in the afternoons, had relaxed conversations with friends and acquaintances, and attended patriotic celebrations at the various legations, consulates, and embassies. They enjoyed "tiffin" at each other's houses and kept careful track of the birthdays and anniversaries that provided such good excuses for a get-together or a party. Life as a foreigner in pre-war Japan was pretty nice while it lasted.

CHAPTER SIX

Home in Japan:
Part Two – 1937, 1938

Ethel had begun keeping diaries when she first married. She recorded events and social engagements in her daily life in tiny handwriting on thin blue paper that still crackles after seventy years. The little leather-bound diaries with "The Blue Funnel Line" embossed in gold on the covers give a picture of her life. They contain very little about international events and very few philosophical reflections or personal insights. Most days, they recount mundane errands and events: what was eaten for dinner, who came for tea, what the weather was like. Many notations were made in her shorthand, indecipherable to this day. But careful reading reveals much by implication.

On 17 April 1937 Ethel recorded that the Taft cake she had made that morning would keep until the next day for her lunch guests. Her cooking repertoire was extensive, but most of the time she made desserts, or one of the Swiss specialties that Hans adored – spaetzle, or fondue. Her Bavarian cream and prune whip were scrumptious, and her baking – date muffins, apple-hazelnut tart, butterscotch pie – was renowned. The cook usually made the main dishes, the amah served them, and Ethel and Hans and their frequent guests would polish off the dessert. She enjoyed those rare occasions when the servants were sick, as long as it was not serious and did not last too long; such times gave her a brief chance to feel in charge again, competent in the kitchen the way her mother had taught her to be back home in Saskatchewan.

In March 1937 Ethel learned that she was pregnant again. As the months of her pregnancy slowly passed she recorded more and more quiet evenings at home in her diary, often by herself when Hans was out with the boys. On weekends, after sailing or rowing in a regatta, the Swiss would celebrate together over a few beers, or play Jass and sing songs that made them all homesick. They got home late, and Ethel, whose life was becoming more circum-scribed, wished that she could have joined them. She usually went to bed early.

She was thirty-one and her health had always been good. Her body had never kept her from doing anything she wanted to do. Most days now she took a long nap in the afternoon, or sat in the sunshine out in the garden. In May she was put on calcium sup-plements and cod liver oil, which she continued until November. On two occasions she nearly fainted in the street and had to take taxis to Dr Coolican's office, where she rested for an hour or so. After the second episode Hans and a good friend, Hammy (short for his last name, Hamilton), took her to the Odeon. They saw *Gorgeous Hussy*, about the political troubles of President Andrew Jackson, starring Lionel Barrymore and Joan Crawford. Afterward they talked about it over nice juicy steaks.

There was an earthquake on 5 May – nothing too serious, but definitely noticeable. Japan's earthquakes had always disturbed Ethel, who liked to have more control over her environment – standing at the top of the stairs and watching the banister shake was unsettling. On her third wedding anniversary, a week later, she and Hans read over their marriage vows, an annual tradition that lasted throughout their life together.

Without servants they could not have lived as they did. If they were invited out for lunch (also known as "tiffin," a Raj term), or dinner, tea, or cocktails, Ethel could simply go. The servants took care of everything at home. When they invited friends over she and the cook decided on the menu, she would make one of her specialties, and that was the end of her responsibilities. Hans loved her cooking, and gave her a "nice jam pot" on her official birthday of 25 June. Her real birthday was at an inconvenient time – Christmas Day – so she always celebrated it six months later. Her birthday parties were renowned because of her baking and homemade jams – red currant and cherry, gooseberry, raspberry, even apricot – and June was fruit season. When visitors dropped in for tea or came to call with little warning, there was always buttered toast with a selection of jams, or Taft or angel food cake. In June of 1937 Ethel's cook took another position, and her replacement "doesn't know beans about cooking." Ethel soon discovered that she didn't know beans about English either.

For Father's Day, 1937, she bought Hans two pipes. In return he took her to the Imperial Hotel for a "delightful concert" that included a "thrilling" new symphony by Wingate. Dinner after was at Lohmeyer's, just the two of them. The newsreel they saw the next evening at the Odeon was all about the coronation of George VI, an event that made all their British friends very happy after that disgraceful business of Edward VIII's abdication in 1936 before his coronation so that he could marry a twice-divorced Mrs Wallis Simpson. Like most of her friends Ethel disapproved of Mrs Simpson for being seductive and disrupting the royal succession, but she secretly admired her for getting what she wanted. They all admired her chic, her clothes, and her hairstyles and tried to look like her.

The previous month Hans had won the Coronation Cup at the boat club, held in honour of the event. Sir Robert Craigie, the British ambassador, had presented it to him, an elegant elongated lozenge-shaped cup in heavy silver to which an enameled Union Jack had been affixed. Hans also won the British Cup that year, sailing alone. Max Pestalozzi won the Swedish Cup in May, sailing in Hans's boat. Vi Woodbridge won the President's Cup, and good old Moke (short for another last name, Mocock) won the Sir Robert Clives Challenge Cup. It was especially nice for him, because he was preparing to go home soon to England. So most of their closest friends won something. Nobody won the German Cup because the race kept being postponed.

On 19 June their boat club entertained members of the Japanese boat club. On such occasions some members stayed away from the club, since the differences of race and social class were more than they could stand. Hans did not share their feelings and had a fine time with their Japanese guests.

The summer of 1937 was hot, as most summers were in Japan. One evening in August Hans and Ethel had dinner together at the Roof Garden restaurant of the New Grand Hotel. It was still extremely hot at 8:00 P.M., but at least there were fewer mosquitoes on the roof. Ethel perspired "terribly" and had her hair cut short the next day so that she could feel cooler. In September Ethel took the train up to Karuizawa with Mrs Hammie to get away from the oppressive heat for a few days. Her friend Christine's baby arrived, which scared Ethel considerably. That night Hans dreamt that Ethel left him, which scared both of them.

Events in Japan were becoming more disturbing towards the end of 1937. Ethel was a foreigner, vulnerable, and separated by many thousands of miles from familiar things, in a country that was, it was becoming clear, using its military might to bully others and assert a new position in the world. Japan had already invaded Manchuria and China. For Ethel, as for most foreigners, life in Japan was manageable as long as she could cover its strangeness with a cloak of familiarity, a cloak that hid the things she did not understand, or that made her afraid. Her friends were English-speaking foreigners, white people who lived in houses and neighbourhoods that could have been Canadian. They went to American movies. They paid Japanese servants to cook like Canadians or Swiss. But by late 1937 the cloak was wearing thin.

In September Ethel was beginning the third trimester of her pregnancy, a time when even the most self-sufficient women often feel vulnerable. On 19 September Ethel's diary read, "Got something in my eye after breakfast. It hurt desperately all day. Couldn't give Vi and Flossie tea. Bought Murine. Lunch at Café Superior in spite of the eye. To bed with it still hurting." There are no more entries in the diary until 18 October, when Professor Miyashita in Tokyo performed the first operation on her eye, followed by a second on 27 October. Thus began a series of ominous events that were to change Ethel's life:

1 November: "Membrane (the conjunctiva, but possibly the cornea itself) broke, and I thought the eye had exploded."
7 November: "New medicine, broke dropper – scared stiff."
8 November: "Skin around the eye broke."
9 November: "Dr Stedefeld cauterized the eye. Said I must have a nurse."
11 November: "Cauterization worked! Abscess stopped. Treatment now simple."
12 November: "Got nurse but don't need her. So glad! Eye improving rapidly."
15 November: "To Tokyo once more – only for Prof. M. to see it, though. Very tired. Eye much better, but needs a long time yet. I am very thin."
16 November: "Dr Stedefeld says I may get up. Cheers! Eight weeks (in bed) is a long time."

Ronald (who immediately became Roni, with a sort of Swiss spelling) was born a few hours after Ethel got up, at 1:55 A.M. on 18 November, at the new International General Hospital of Yokohama, during a week of blackouts in preparation for air raids. He was only the second baby born in the hospital. At seven pounds nine ounces he was perfectly healthy, even if his mother was not. There were no more diary entries until 8 February 1938, when a nurse came because Ethel was sick with flu. By 25 February she was well enough to attend a recital (Beethoven's "Kreutzer" Sonata) at the International Women's Club with a Swiss friend, Max Pestalozzi, who came for lunch and stayed to tea. Vi joined her for dinner. On 12 March she saw her first movie in six months – *Ten Men and a Girl* with Deanna Durbin. She "could see it quite

Arai-san holding Roni in 1938.

well." The next day Vi, Kitty, and Marcus Weidmann, another Swiss friend who had always carried a torch for her, visited all at once, and she brought Roni out so that he could be admired. By this time Ethel was getting back to her social round of lunches, teas, and cocktail parties, but it was a strain; she complained of "too much sociability for my eyes." On 1 April she was fitted for a new blue dress by Monique, her favourite dressmaker, and wore it the next weekend to a party at the Swiss legation in Tokyo. Once again, the party was a "bit too much" for her eyes and even the new dress did not help.

Dr Stedefeld told Ethel not to be too optimistic about her eye, which spoiled her day. She had to have another operation to close the hole in her cornea, and Dr Coolican insisted that it was time to wean Roni because she had to look after her eye. So on 2 May she put belladonna plasters on her nipples, feeling absolutely awful about denying "poor wee Roni." She "had lots (of milk) for him" but had to wear a tight binder in an effort to diminish the supply. Marcus came to visit one May afternoon while Roni was cooing to himself in his pram out in the garden—he was always such a good baby. He confided to the distraught young mother that his own mother had finally weaned him when he was four years old. Feeling a bit out of his depth, Marcus suggested that they see *Double Wedding* that evening with Max and Hans and go out after to the Hamburg Bar. Ethel was happy to be able to join them again, since she no longer provided Roni's supper. The servants could now feed him.

On 24 May Ethel had yet another operation in Tokyo with more follow-up because the hole in the cornea still had not closed properly. She could not be there on the twenty-ninth when Hans won the British Cup, sailing alone, but at least she could join them after the race. Another operation on 17 June still didn't make it right. It was a bad time – Roni was feverish, pale and wan, Hans was in the hospital with some kind of infection, and the roads to Tokyo were awash with heavy rains. Thank goodness for staunch friends like Vi, who came and stayed with Ethel for a few days. Marcus visited daily, looking a bit like a lovestruck schoolboy, and often they all went to the movies together. On 25 August 1938 Ethel recorded that the servants were all "required to attend some kind of mass meeting," so she stayed home with Roni and made brownies; she felt "happy." The servants came home after the meeting and never disclosed its purpose to Ethel.

By the end of August 1938 Roni had three teeth and was crawling around the house. There was a violent typhoon on the thirtieth that left the garden a mess and the electricity out, but the race at the boat club was held afterward – for boats that still had masts.

There was a party at the club on 22 September but only twenty people were there. Earlier that day Ethel had an appointment with Dr Stedefeld, who recommended yet another eye operation. This presented her with more to worry about as she prepared the dressings to cover her eye every night. The doctor wanted her to have the operation in Switzerland, which led to a meeting between Dr Stedefeld and Hans's boss, Mr Nipkow. They all agreed that she should travel to Switzerland before Hans went on home leave, especially since the war scare in Europe seemed to be subsiding by late September 1938. After a consultation with Dr Miyashita (whose opinion was crucial for her travel plans) Ethel's mind was made up, but she "felt pretty blue about it." Why had all this happened to her?

Her passage with Roni was booked for early November, and for the next month they had dinner guests nearly every night, unless they were invited out. There were parties every weekend. Hans started going in to the office on Sundays and Ethel walked with him to keep him company. On the face of it life seemed fine, but there were disturbing things beneath the surface, like the mysterious meetings the servants had to attend. It was all oddly symbolized, somehow, by something that happened on 29 September. Vi was the coxswain in a regatta for a "four" that included Hans. They rammed a submerged pole and the boat sank. It produced a certain amount of merriment among the onlookers and a great deal of embarrassment for Vi, who was not really responsible. The boat was a wreck. On 9 October Ethel went for a walk in the full moon before dinner. "My last in Japan? I wonder …"

On 5 November she and Roni departed for Vancouver on the SS *Empress of Russia* at 3:00 P.M. Hans carried the whimpering baby up the gangplank to their cabin. There were no festive streamers this time. Heavy weather was forecast, and when Hans appeared with the baby the captain himself was helping to tie down Roni's cot. There were stout ropes at each corner so that it would not come adrift and ricochet around Ethel's cabin when the ship was pitching and rolling. Having the captain checking on things was reassuring. But Ethel felt afraid and overwhelmed. Here she was, about to travel across the Pacific Ocean alone with her one-year-old baby, and able to see only half of what she was accustomed to seeing. The prospect of a rough crossing was not encouraging, although she had become a fairly good sailor and was not much concerned about seasickness. Still, there were no more diary entries for many weeks.

CHAPTER SEVEN

Home Leave in the Wrong Place – 1939

Ethel's eye patch was there to stay, but only, she hoped, until one of the specialists in New York or Zurich could restore the vision in her right eye. She was filled with dread – about her vision, about her physical appearance, about leaving her husband, and about the situation in Europe, her destination. She was also concerned about the situation in Japan, the home she was leaving. The military now appeared to be running the country, and uniforms were everywhere.

Adding to her worries, an American friend had begged her to carry his Winchester rifle and six hundred rounds of ammunition back to the States for him. It was all in one of her trunks, and a luggage inspection could have gotten her into serious trouble with the military authorities. Fortunately, the Japanese inspectors on the pier did not open her bags and trunks. People going abroad for a year had a lot of bags, but x-ray scanning was not used on luggage in those days. So she was safe.

A week later her basic honesty made her declare the Winchester on the Canadian customs form as the ship approached Vancouver harbour. It turned out that the customs inspector was an old friend from her school days in Regina. The first thing he said to her on the pier when she landed was, "All I need to see is that 'G-U-N'." So it was temporarily confiscated, checked over by the police, and delivered to her in Regina a couple of weeks later complete with ammunition, which in 1939 was already useless. Her little brother Harvey tried to use it for shooting gophers – a favourite pastime of young men on the prairies. To the good fortune of the gophers, at least half of the shells were duds.

After the difficulties and anxieties of the previous year, Ethel was relieved to be at home, once again in the bosom of her family. Sitting in the parlour after supper, surrounded by her kin and sewing by the light of a kerosene lamp – after her years abroad it was almost too good to be true. The familiar sound of the wind howling outside was welcome, even when the temperature dropped well below zero. She could relax for a few months as long as she knew that Hans was safe in her other home, on the other side of the globe.

Her younger sister Muriel wanted nothing more than to look after her baby nephew and show him off to all the friends and neighbours who came to visit. Ethel's parents were happy and thankful to have her safely under their own roof once again, especially at Christmastime. They had never travelled to Japan during the seven years she had been there. Not one of her family ever visited Ethel abroad. She did not know whether it was the expense, the time, their fear of the mysterious Orient, or a feeling that they did not belong there. It was as if she had sailed out of their lives and dropped off the edge of their world. Her trip to the eye doctor in New York was nothing in comparison. She was still in North America. But now she had returned, with a patch over her eye from an infection she had gotten across the sea in Japan – the prodigal daughter.

Ethel was acutely aware of the change in her appearance. She was still in her thirties, but her eye patch made her feel disfigured. Her friends and family still loved her, as they always had, and reassured her that they did not even notice the patch. They were happy to take her shopping or drive her to childhood haunts, or help her in any way they could. Roni was a big hit – a healthy, happy baby whose teething troubles were now much better. Like most babies he spent a lot of time contentedly gazing up at his admirers, none of whom were Japanese any more.

Ethel was very concerned with Roni's appearance and used to tape his ears back so that they would not stick out. This practice did not strike her as at all unusual, although to modern mothers it probably seems barbaric. Roni was fond of sucking his thumb, and his toes too if he got a chance. She was desperately afraid that he would develop buckteeth from thumb sucking, so she tried to prevent it by fastening cardboard sleeves around his chubby little arms or putting ill-tasting potions on his thumbs. These did not go over well with Roni, but they did stop the thumb-sucking. Child-rearing practices were very different in the 1930s.

Hans left Yokohama on 16 March 1939 and reached Richardson on the twenty-seventh. The tang of cold deep snow pervaded the outside air, while the smell of wet wool and woodsmoke filled the inside. For three weeks they lived on the farm, Hans helping with the chores and doing a lot of errands in Grandpa Kyle's Buick. He was not used to the icy roads and was very worried about ending up in a ditch. He did not venture out at night. Ethel managed to do some of the cooking again. It was a fine respite for all of them, far from their accustomed routines in Yokohama. They all went to the little church in Richardson on Sunday mornings and wondered how long peace would last. The signs in Europe were growing more and more ominous. That was where they were going next.

On 16 April they left on the Canadian Pacific transcontinental train for Montreal. From there they went to New York, where they boarded the SS *Rex* of the Italian Line. Roni was very popular with the ship's staff because of his love of pasta and his jolly temperament. Hans's sisters Berti and Martha were waiting on the Italian Line pier in Genoa to welcome them home. There was also a chorus of men wearing the distinctive black shirts of the Italian Fascist uniform singing a welcome to a returning official in

Hans, Ethel, and Roni on board the Italian liner *Rex*, leaving from New York for Europe on 24 April 1939.

Mussolini's government. When Hans had lived in Milan during the twenties, the "blackshirts" had not seemed so menacing, but now they posed a very real threat.

The train trip up to Zurich was uneventful except at the Italian-Swiss border, where Italian soldiers were much in evidence around Domodossola. On the Swiss side, Ethel and Hans saw ominous preparations for demolition of the St Gotthard Tunnel. The Swiss were determined not to become a thoroughfare through which the Nazis and their Italian Fascist allies would travel. All of the major roads and bridges in Switzerland now had dynamite under them, ready for demolition if the bigger, more warlike countries to the north, east, and south invaded the country. Switzerland's neutrality had been maintained since Napoleonic times, during more than a century of warfare among her neighbours on all sides. It had become a sacred matter, an integral part of the Swiss identity. It was maintained by what they called the "Porcupine Principle," which meant relying on the country's forbidding geography, and being armed to the teeth and ready to repel invaders, whether they came from Germany, Austria, Italy, or France.

Hans and Ethel arrived in the village of Erlenbach on 2 May 1939, just in time for the blossoms on Frau Bänninger's fruit trees. It was the loveliest month of the year along the shores of the Lake of Zurich, and a time when young couples with new babies should have been happy and carefree. Hans and Ethel were surrounded by loving friends and relatives, even if the country was tense. Hans spoke his native language again from morning until night, and Ethel realized how relaxed and happy that made him, whatever the Nazis had in mind. He always seemed to be the life of the party, full of bonhomie – Gemütlichkeit – once again, the way he had been when she first met him in Japan.

A week later, on a damp spring morning, Hans and Ethel set the alarm early and got up to make the half-hour train journey from Erlenbach into Zurich, leaving Roni at home with the family. Surrounded by mountains on three sides and with its sizable lake in the middle, Zurich does not have an agreeable or healthy climate, and as they looked blearily down from the rail line just above the shores of the Lake of Zurich on their way into town, all Ethel and Hans could see was a sort of smoky mist where they knew the lake was, and the sodden grey brown stucco and cement of the many villas and hotels that backed up along its shores on what is today called the "Gold Coast," where only the wealthy can afford to live.

The train arrived at the Bahnhof in Zurich right on the dot, as they usually do in Switzerland, and Hans and Ethel were on schedule as they emerged from the station. The blue-and-white trams moved silently up and down the Bahnhofstrasse, and the air smelled of damp electricity from the trolleys' overhead wires, mixed with the odours of coal, cabbage, and urban mildew. The moist air seemed full of foreboding and *tristesse*.

It would not have felt like a festive day under the best of circumstances, but Ethel and Hans were feeling particularly in tune with the gloomy surroundings today because they were on their way to see yet another eye specialist, the latest in what began to seem like a hopeless campaign to do something to improve Ethel's vision and appearance.

This time, they were off to see a Dr Vogt at his office in Zurich. He was an internationally famous ophthalmologist, one of the few doctors in the world capable of performing surgery that might actually help Ethel to regain at least some of the sight in her right eye.

It was not a long tramride to the doctor's offices, up the hill near the Kantonsspital, and they entered the discreetly luxurious waiting room half an hour before the appointment. Ethel had become obsessive about being early, even before arriving in time-conscious, watch-ridden Switzerland. It made her feel more in control, with a better chance of coming out ahead in a world where everything – from her vision and appearance to the outlook for international peace – seemed to be going straight to hell. In any case, the waiting room was warm and comfortable, and it was interesting to watch the other patients who came from all over the world to see the renowned doctor.

Everyone in the waiting room looked up when a very large man dressed entirely in black, with a full-length leather coat, a fedora, and dark glasses, walked out of the doctor's consultation room. This coarse bull of an individual walked straight through the waiting room to the door, accompanied by two sullen, thuggish men who had been seated inconspicuously in the corner.

Ethel was ushered into Dr Vogt's office next, leaving Hans in the waiting room, contentedly reading his hometown newspapers. After the initial introductions and courtesies, Dr Vogt told Ethel in excellent English that the man who had just left was Signor

Mussolini, who had flown up from Rome the night before for an emergency consultation. But whereas the doctor had had to tell Mussolini that his infection, which was due to syphilis, could not be treated, he assured Ethel that with a bit of luck, she could make a full recovery.

This was the first encouraging thing Ethel had heard for quite a while, and the trip home with Hans, particularly after the glass of champagne they had drunk at a hotel bar near the station, was a good deal less tense than the ride in. They even thought of staying in town for lunch, but Ethel wanted to get back to Erlenbach to see to her little boy. Roni was one and a half by now, but he still seemed like a novelty, and he was one of the few happy things in Ethel's life during those difficult days.

In the following weeks Ethel underwent three separate eye operations performed by Dr Vogt at the Rotkreuzspital in Zurich. Between the second and third she had to lie perfectly still for an entire week, since even the slightest movement or shock could jeopardize the regaining of her sight.

In early August, Dr Vogt was finally able to tell them that the hole in Ethel's cornea was now closed and the pressure on the eyeball was back to normal. Her vision had not been restored, but the eye was stable and she was free to leave. She no longer needed to wear an eye patch or even glasses; but Ethel did not want people to see her tattooed iris and decided to wear dark glasses most of the time, both outdoors and in.

That summer of 1939 was a happy time, despite the pervasive anxiety about the world situation. Roni was learning to speak two languages at once. Though he had been exposed to English from birth, he was actually becoming better at Schwyzer-Tütsch, the Swiss-German dialect. He was fed lots of fine Swiss chocolate by his doting relatives. An early and stalwart walker, he was allowed to pick cherries off the tree in Grossmutti's backyard. He was, after all, her first and only grandchild and there was a lot of separation time to make up for. There were picnics and splashing in the lake, and his uncles and aunts conspired to spoil him rotten.

On 18 June Roni was christened in the little church on the lakeshore in Erlenbach. Schaggi and Berti, Hans's older brother and sister, served as godparents. Each of them gave Roni a five-franc piece, the old silver ones with William Tell on one side. Berti had driven down from Appenzell, where she lived with her husband, Walter Blatter, high in the hills in the town of Walzenhausen. Walter was a little gnome of a man with a happy smile and no wish to travel far from his mountain home. That was just as well, since his elderly Opel was a real rattletrap. But down they came, and Walter even wore a tie for the occasion.

In July the Landes Ausstellung opened in Zurich. This was the really big Swiss National Exposition, held every twenty-five years, and it was supposed to remain open until October. The "Landi" began with a big parade through the streets of Zurich, and the whole city turned out to celebrate Switzerland and its place in the world. More than a hundred different local and cantonal costumes were worn by the marchers, and there were bands and musicians from all regions of the country, including speakers of Romansch, one of the four languages of the country, from eastern Switzerland. There were yodellers and alphorn blowers, championship soccer teams and gymnasts from many regions of Switzerland, and lots of *Fahnenschwingen* (flag-tossing), in which flags are thrown high in the air with such skill that they twist and spin before being caught again, creating a wonderful hula effect. The Baenninger family went several times, trying to soak everything in – the technical, agricultural, and manufacturing exhibits, the music and the food; all the astonishing diversity of a country that measured about two hundred miles long and barely a hundred miles wide.

Hans and Ethel went out for dinners with their friends Fritz and Elsa Locher and visited their house on the lake in Küsnacht. Fritz had been one of Hans's messmates in Japan. Now an officer in the Swiss army, he anticipated being called up before very long. Where Fritz was handsome and charming, Elsa was talented, athletic, and beautiful. They both spoke English very well, which made them good company for Ethel. The Baenningers and Lochers drove up into the mountains in Fritz's new cream-coloured American convertible, over the Gotthard Pass, and to the Vierwaldstädtersee, the Rigi, and Luzern. It was a magical time, the summer of 1939.

Nazi Germany, across Lake Constance, grew more menacing with each passing day. Everything still looked normal. Steamers crossed back and forth on the lake, some flying the German swastika, others the white cross on a red background, the flag of Switzerland. There was music on weekends from the restaurants and beer halls on both sides of the lake. In the light of the setting sun, with the sound of yodelling or choral singing drifting across the water, war seemed unthinkable. Everywhere the church bells rang out on Saturday evenings, and the profound lowing of alphorns could sometimes be heard.

But high above the lake on the Swiss side gun emplacements were secretly being constructed in the hillsides, many of them inside picturesque chalets. Behind flowers in the window boxes the huge barrels of Swiss long-range artillery were aimed toward Friedrichshafen, where German factories were churning out war materiel for the Third Reich. Near Walzenhausen, and all over Switzerland (once Hans and Ethel began to notice them), there were concrete tank traps strategically placed in valleys, streambeds, and gullies. About one metre high, these unsightly but effective devices were designed to stop the tanks of invading armies by dislocating their treads. All along Switzerland's borders with Germany and Austria preparations for national defence were underway.

The Swiss knew that a serious onslaught by the armies of the Third Reich would succeed eventually, but they meant to discourage the invaders as far as they could and put up a good fight before they were overrun. They hoped that the prospect of their prolonged resistance would deter the Germans. During World War I the German kaiser had inspected the Swiss army on manoeuvres that were held for his benefit. When the kaiser pointed out that his army was twice as big as the Swiss army and demanded to know what they would do about that, a Swiss officer suggested that he and his men would just have to shoot twice as often. In fact they did. The Swiss developed a machine gun called the Oerlikon gun, which both sides bought from them under license during the war.

A modern, well-prepared Swiss air force was equipped with French fighter planes that could take off on short notice from airstrips hidden in the mountains. Pilots could not go very far in a straight line before turning back because the longest distance across the country, from the French border near Geneva to the German border in the east, was only two hundred miles, about thirty minutes in a fast fighter plane. There was, of course, no Swiss navy, Switzerland being a landlocked country. The half-million men in the Swiss army were well trained and fully equipped to defend their homeland.

The "home field advantage" is important in warfare, just as it is in sports. A citizens' army, or militia, had been a Swiss institution for many years, during peacetime and wartime, and they knew how to get around in wild terrain that was often nearly vertical. Every able-bodied Swiss man went for six months of military training when he turned twenty. Those who lived abroad, like Hans, or who were ineligible had to pay a hefty military tax (a flat one percent of gross income) in lieu of military service. All Swiss men between the ages of twenty and fifty-two put in two weeks a year of *Militärdienst* marching, target-shooting, equipment maintenance, and whatever else was necessary to keep the army battle-ready. There was only one general, General Guisan, who was as close to a national hero as the Swiss have had since William Tell (who also stood up against foreign invaders).

For most men military duty was not a hardship. Their employers allowed them two weeks off with full pay every year, in addition to their vacation time. Each year they put on their uniforms, got their army rifles, bayonets, helmets, and marching gear out of the cupboard (they also had live ammunition stored in their homes), and went off to staging areas all over the country. Usually they were out in the country or up in the mountains with men they knew, eating good, healthy meals, drinking copious quantities of

Swiss wine and schnapps, and getting lots of exercise. Groups of soldiers, often singing in chorus as they marched along the roads, were a common sight all over Switzerland. They knew they were doing their patriotic duty, that it was important for maintaining Swiss neutrality, and that they were part of an organization that held the nation together. In some ways it was like the Boy Scouts, but it was deadly serious.

On 1 September 1939 the Germans invaded Poland. The shock was felt all over Europe, and Switzerland mobilized immediately. By nine o'clock the following morning Hans's brother Schaggi had to report for duty in Affoltern-am-Albis, where they had grown up and where their father had been the village policeman. On that Sunday morning there was no way to get there by train from Erlenbach, which was across the Lake of Zurich on the other side of the Uetliberg – not exactly a mountain, but not a molehill either. Hans had to go too, so that he could drive his brother's old Wolseley back to Erlenbach. He had never had a driving license for Switzerland, but anybody who had a Shanghai driving license in the 1930s and had survived was obviously daring, lucky, and capable of facing Swiss traffic on Mobilization Day – even in an unfamiliar car. Just as they were about to leave, Schaggi discovered that the Wolseley had a flat tire. After changing it they managed to arrive in Affoltern with five minutes to spare, so there was hardly time to say goodbye as Schaggi went bounding off to join his regiment. Hans managed to get back to Erlenbach without incident and without a second flat tire, which would have reduced him to walking since he had no spare. Police were directing traffic in parts of Zurich, something that was highly unusual in peacetime.

The next morning Hans showed up bright and early at the military command centre (the Kreiskommando) in Erlenbach to see if he was needed, or expected to report for any kind of wartime duty. He was told, rather abruptly, that *Auslandschweizer* (the Swiss who lived abroad) should immediately return to wherever they came from and wait there until the war was over. In Switzerland they were simply more mouths to feed. At that moment, when he was told to leave his native land, Hans felt truly homeless. Japan was where he lived, but he had never really thought of it as home. And Canada was Ethel's home, not his.

But even getting to Canada might prove difficult. The people at the American Express office in Zurich told Hans that his reservations on the *Rex* had been summarily cancelled. The ship was staying in port at Genoa until further notice. It seemed like a crazy action for the Italian Line to take. A lot of people were fleeing Europe in the fall of 1939, especially Jewish refugees, and they were willing to pay anything for tickets to New York. Fortunately, the ss *Vulcania* still had some space for those who had held reservations on the *Rex*. It cost one hundred dollars extra for each of them and they were assigned a very small cabin near the engine room down on D deck. But they had their tickets, their visas were in order, and they were leaving on 23 September. Their panic subsided and they resigned themselves to the extortion. In the years to come it seemed like a bargain.

The *Vulcania* was jammed with people of many nationalities escaping Europe. They were camping out in parts of the cargo hold, prepared to live on mattresses. The ship made an unscheduled stop in Lisbon to pick up more mattresses, and another large group of frightened refugees from Germany and France. Some of them had to sleep on deck. But there seemed to be limitless quantities of spaghetti, cooked in every imaginable style. With enough to eat, a place to sleep, and the prospect of safety in America at the end of their voyage, the *Vulcania*'s passengers knew that things were improving. Roni charmed the Italian waiters by regularly asking for more pasta in a two-year-old's version of Italian.

The Baenningers were not stopping in America. They were going home to Japan and visiting Regina en route. Since their baggage was marked "in transit," they had no trouble with it on the pier in New York, though Hans's new accordian caused an incident at customs. Bought in Switzerland, it was the kind with buttons only, no piano keys, and was excellent for playing Swiss tunes – the lively laendlers, schottisches, marches, and polkas that would cheer up any room full of Swiss, and most non-Swiss too. After questioning Hans for a bit, the American customs inspector remarked that he had never seen an accordian like that and told Hans to play it for him. So Hans had to pull up a stool and play a Swiss song or two on the New York pier, surrounded by a large audience of European refugees. Everyone was amused by the impromptu recital, and some of those from German-speaking countries looked a little nostalgic. The inspector thanked Hans and marked the accordion "in transit" so that he would not have to pay customs duty.

A cab took the Baenningers and their luggage to Grand Central Station, where they boarded the train for Montreal. They wound their way up through the Hudson River valley, catching glimpses of the distant Adirondack Mountains and Lake Champlain. The autumn apple harvest was in progress, and it was wonderful to admire beautiful scenery that was not marred by tank traps. They spent a night at the Windsor Hotel in Montreal, right beside the smoky railroad station, and then set off for Regina. Canadian Pacific trains were still the best way to cross the country in 1939, and the long maroon train was crowded as it snaked along behind its big black steam locomotive past Ottawa and the Parliament Buildings, through Sudbury, with its vast nickel mines, and on through the endless forests to the north of Lake Huron and Lake Superior. After brief stops in Fort William and Port Arthur to take on coal and water for the boilers, they continued on past Lake of the Woods to Winnipeg. The immense flat wheat fields of the Canadian prairies that began in Manitoba reminded Hans and Ethel of being at sea. Finally, after more than two days in their cozy travelling compartment, the train arrived at the downtown railroad station in Regina, a little more than halfway to Vancouver.

Ethel's parents were still on the farm in Richardson and moved into Regina only after the war. It felt about as far from Erlenbach as they could imagine, but in the middle of this enormous, sparsely-populated country, everything felt unnaturally safe. Once again, they were surrounded by warm, loving relatives, who now spoke

English instead of Swiss-German. For the first time in many years the entire Kyle family celebrated Thanksgiving together, relieved and happy to have Ethel and her husband and child safely out of Europe.

Roni had cousins to play with, Mavis and Larry and Wayne, who were close to him in age. His uncle Harvey, still a teenager, was fascinated that Roni could speak Swiss-German better than English. He had never heard anyone, grownup or child, speak another language. When Roni said that his mother's teapot felt *heiss*, Harvey thought he said "ice" and decided that his nephew was very peculiar – certainly different from Canadian kids, all of whom found teapots hot. Cousin Mavis kept grinning at Hans and holding up her hands; he finally figured out that she thought they represented his name.

Hans and Ethel were booked on the *Empress of Canada*, which was leaving Vancouver early in November. Despite a lot of subtle hints from her family, they were firm in their resolve to return to Japan. So once again they boarded the Canadian Pacific train, bound for a nation that would be at war with Canada in two years. The Rockies were spectacular, as usual, and there were more relatives in Vancouver to visit. Their departure was delayed for a couple of days while a large gun was installed on the *Empress's* rear deck. Hans was puzzled by it. These were dangerous times, but there were no German submarines in the Pacific, and Japan was not at war with anyone yet. And why was the gun facing aft?

It was a peaceful voyage. They crossed the International Date Line, the point at which, if you were travelling east, it suddenly became the previous day. They arrived in Yokohama on Roni's birthday, 18 November, which was always celebrated on the seventeenth by the relatives in Canada, since that was the day they got the news. There was a combined farewell and birthday party for Roni, now two, and all the kids onboard, complete with little sandwiches and ice cream and cake. Thanks to the festivities, they had to wait before going down the gangplank, but eventually their feet were back on Japanese soil. Getting through customs

CHILDREN'S TEA PARTY

John Ashworth	Sheila Morphew
Ronald Baenninger	Hilary Morphew
Jacqueline Breen	Patrick Mulvaney
Duncan Boyars	Jane Roberts
David Girling	Charles Roberts
Eva Hansen	John Roberts
Erik Hansen	Michael Roberts
Sheila Harrop	George Scott
Arthur Hill	Harry Scott
Ronald Hillman	Gillian Sherwin
Renee Hubert	William Stoker
Elizabeth Hubert	Cynthia Trent
Marcia Hubert	Patricia Trent
Josette Hubert	Ronald Wells-Henderson
Daphne Hutchison	David Wevil
Penelope Hutchison	Hilary Wevil
Richard Jones	Hilary Whitley
Robin Jones	Winifred Williams
Bryan Lewis	Janet Williams
David Lewis	Heather Williams

R.M.S. "Empress of Canada"
At Sea
Wednesday, 8th November, 1939

MENU

Orange Cocktail

Sandwiches:-

Chicken   Ham   Lettuce

Jam   Eggs

Gateau Canadian Pacific

Strawberry Melba

French Pastries

Fudge   Chocolates

Tea   Cocoa   Milk

Menu for a children's tea party (a daily event) on the Canadian Pacific liner *Empress of Canada*.

Canadian Pacific

EMPRESS OF CANADA

BREAKFAST

Yeast Cakes
Grape Fruit   Melon   Pomeloe
Iced Juices: Prune   Papaia   Clam

Stewed Figs   Compote of Prunes

Oatmeal Porridge   Rolled Oats   Creamed Semolina
All Bran   Corn Flakes   Puffed Wheat
Post Toasties   Rice Krispies

Fried Silver Bream, Orly
Fish Cakes, Anchovy Sauce

Eggs: Boiled   Fried   Turned   Poached   Scrambled
Omelettes: Plain   Parsley   Tomato

Broiled Windsor Back Bacon
Saute of Kidney Turbigo
Lyonnaised Potatoes

GRILL AND TO ORDER
Small Steak, Straw Potatoes
Grilled Canadian Ham

COLD SELECTION
Roast Lamb, Mint Sauce   Boar's Head
Galantine of Veal
Watercress   Radishes

ROLLS AND BREADS
Vienna Rolls   Graham Rolls
Almond Muffins   Bran Muffins
Cinnamon Buns   Oat Cakes
Toasts: Plain,   Buttered,   Melba,   Brown,   Cinnamon
Breads: White, Brown, Raisin, Malt
Buckwheat Cakes with Syrup

Conserves   Marmalade

Coffee: Kona and American

Cocoa   Tea
Buttermilk

Saturday, November 18th 1939   .T.

Passengers on Special Diet are requested to inform the Head Waiter of their requirements

A more lavish prewar menu from the Empress of Canada, *stamped in honour of Roni's second birthday.*

took a long time. Grim-faced agents stringently checked all the bags and trunks, and the whole atmosphere at the customs and immigration shed seemed much less friendly and welcoming than in the past. Still, Hans had been away for nine months and Ethel and Roni for almost a year, and they were glad to be back.

CHAPTER EIGHT

Back to Japan and a Deteriorating Outlook – 1940

After a week or so of unpacking and homecoming parties, life resumed its usual tempo. Everyone was curious to hear Hans and Ethel's fresh news from Europe and their up-to-the-minute impressions of a continent going to war: what did they think Germany was going to do next? Compared to what they had just left in Europe, life in Japan seemed pretty normal at first, except that a lot of American and British women gradually seemed to be vanishing. Many items that had never been in short supply were becoming scarce, and one had to become more imaginative when shopping for groceries, among other things. Ethel nonetheless continued to do a lot of baking – if anything, more than before – though she sometimes wondered why she went to all the bother. It all began to seem a bit pointless, and yet one had to keep busy somehow. It was a bizarre period during which nobody wanted to openly admit that anything was wrong, but when evidently nothing was quite right, either. People kept up their daily routine in a sort of limbo and with a growing sense of unreality. Hans was particularly busy at work because of all the problems caused by the upheaval in Europe, and Ethel was glad to have Roni as a companion. With his amusing speech and wide-eyed curiosity, he was becoming better and better company.

Hans and Ethel's social life became even busier than before their home leave – almost frantic – as people congregated in an effort to overcome the loneliness of uncertainty. Drinking had always been a popular pastime in the social flutter of the Far East, but many people now found themselves consuming more alcohol, in spite of their best intentions. Imported liquor was still available, and Hans and Ethel often had a gimlet or a martini before dinner – and sometimes two. Familiar faces were missing at the boat club and elsewhere in the social round, but life went on; those remaining simply made all the merrier to make up for those who had departed. There were still Jass evenings about once a month, usually at the club, and the Swiss chef at the New Grand Hotel in Yokohama worked wonders in transforming whatever provisions were available into meals that were still acceptable. But while the setting was still jolly, the service was not what it used to be, and the Japanese help seemed less keen to gratify their foreign clientele.

On many afternoons Ethel and Roni had tea together, just the two of them; Ethel also frequently entertained other ladies, or was entertained by them. None of the women had much to do, and lots of talking and visiting and admiring each other's children kept their minds off the bad things that might lie ahead. Getting a shampoo at the hairdresser's provided another welcome distraction during this long period of suspense, and Ethel thought she probably had the cleanest hair she had ever had in her life. She continued her German lessons as well but found it hard to concentrate and to memorize the difficult grammar and vocabulary. It was a tough language, and it now seemed less desirable to learn than when she had begun. In the meantime, Hans's English had continued to improve during their five years of marriage. It had become almost perfect, to the point where there was really no longer any practical reason for Ethel to learn his mother tongue. Besides, he and his friends spoke mostly Schwytzer-Tütsch the whole time, and Ethel knew enough High German to realize that no amount of study could help her to master an unwritten dialect that waspish French-Swiss and Italian-Swiss often describe as a throat disease.

Shopping became good fun, and Ethel always liked to be well turned out for the social events on their calendar. And the purchase of tangible treasures in troubled times has always been a reassuring way to ward off vague threats, which lack the concreteness of things. The beautiful double strand of Japanese pearls from Mikimoto that Hans bought for Ethel in August was a gorgeous piece of jewellery as well as a shield against calamity.

The institution of marriage provided a similar "guarantee" of security, and during 1940 Hans and Ethel attended more weddings than during any year in their lives. Most of the couples who wed left Japan immediately or soon after tying the knot, but there was something about the precarious environment that caused couples to want to get everything tied down and secured before leaving. Ethel spent a lot of time shopping for presents and then wrapping them, and by the end of the year she tired of weddings.

There were still movies to go to and Hans and Ethel went as often as they could. The dances were still fun, too, although for some reason they seemed to end earlier than they used to and Ethel was disappointed to find herself back home as early as eleven o'clock on some nights. But one invented other distractions. Now that Japan was increasingly cut off from the rest of the world, the coming and going of passenger ships – until then an everyday occurrence that no one took much notice of – gained new interest. Sometimes an acquaintance could be met on incoming ships, bringing fresh news from abroad as well as scarce commodities like flour, sugar, or silk stockings. More often someone was leaving, and on every departing ship there were, sadly, people to whom one had to say goodbye.

After the many crossings they had made over the years, the Baenningers knew most of the Canadian Pacific captains. One of the most personable was Captain Patrick, skipper of the *Empress of Russia*. Ethel sometimes wandered alone down to the docks in the afternoon if she noticed in the port register that his ship was due. She would greet him, perhaps have a cup of tea on the bridge, and hear the latest from the outside. Just being aboard the gently swaying ship for a short while, chatting openly without worrying about listening servants, was a soothing break from Japan and its tense atmosphere. Even the smells of the ship and the sea were relaxing. They reminded Ethel of her own travels and of being elsewhere.

Nature took no notice of the political ups and downs. Earthquakes and typhoons continued to wreak havoc on people of all political persuasions. The boat club premises were badly damaged one night by what the press called a "baby typhoon," and members had to get together to clear up the mess. There was on overwhelming response to the call for volunteers: people seemed glad to rally even to a simple mission like cleaning up the club grounds. It kept their minds off other things.

When people tired of the boat club, they could go to the Alt Heidelberg restaurant where the Japanese waitresses were dressed in Bavarian costumes. The Rheingold Bar in Yokohama was another favourite spot to pass the time. It did not offer full meals, but the draft beer was a treat and the sandwiches were excellent. One regular patron was a handsome middle-aged man who almost always sat at the same corner table nursing a mug of beer, staring straight in front of him, and exuding tragedy. As everyone learned at war's end, this was Richard Sorge, a German journalist who, with the help of a German radio expert, had set up and run a spy ring for the Soviets in the Far East. He lived in Yokohama with his wife, a ballerina. As regional editor of the *Frankfurter Algemeine Zeitung*, Sorge moved in high circles when he wasn't listening to the patter in the Rheingold Bar. He was befriended by the German ambassador and his wife, Herr and Frau vonDirksen. The principal sources of the intelligence he gathered were Japanese Communists in the inner sanctum of Prince Konoye, the prime minister, and Sorge managed to carry on his secret activities undetected, right under the nose of the Nazis and the Japanese secret police, the *Kempeitai*, until 1941, when he was found out and arrested by the Japanese. The high-grade information he obtained proved to be of critical strategic importance to the Russians, especially his advance warning to Stalin in 1940 of Operation Barbarossa, the imminent Nazi invasion of Russia. After the war Richard Sorge emerged posthumously as a famous figure in Russia, the only foreigner ever to be named a "Hero of the Soviet Union" or to have his picture appear on a Russian postage stamp. He would certainly have thought it meagre compensation for the Soviet refusal to trade him for Japanese prisoners during the war. After languishing in prison for three years, Sorge was hanged by the Japanese in late 1944 and is buried in a Japanese graveyard.

Early in 1940, a new cabinet headed by the universally respected Admiral Yonai took over the reins of government. This cabinet announced a policy of "non-involvement" in the European sphere, which, British diplomats were assured in secret briefings, was tantamount to a declaration of neutrality. The regime continued to promote Japanese interests aggressively in all spheres, especially in Southeast Asia, but the government was openly opposed to the warlike stance that the German Reich had long been urging upon Japan. The Yonai cabinet did not constitute a democratic government by Western standards, but it was a big improvement on its more bellicose predecessors and might well have developed along positive lines had events unfolded more favourably for the Allies in Europe.

All kinds of contentious issues arose. In one incident, a British cruiser intercepted a Japanese ship carrying German reservists and technicians who had found themselves stuck in the United States. These men were being repatriated via Japan and the Trans-Siberian Railroad to join Hitler's armed forces. The British judged that transporting enemy troops was inconsistent with Japan's professed "neutrality" and wanted to press home the point. Unfortunately, rough weather delayed the interception of the offending vessel, the ss *Asama Maru*, until it was only thirty-five miles from the Japanese coast. Once it was stopped, British officers boarded the ship and removed twenty-one German "technicians" to the cruiser as prisoners. This was the first time that a Japanese ship had been subjected to a search so close to home, and the incident triggered a violently angry reaction in the press and amongst the populace. Japanese pride had been tweaked and the resolution of the incident kept diplomats on both sides busy for weeks.

Endless arguments about access to the Yangtze River in China for international trade were a further source of friction. By the spring of 1940, the British ambassador had made real headway on this complex and delicate issue thanks to his endless patience and consummate skill at allowing the Japanese, at each stage of the negotiations, to "save face." A breakthrough seemed near. In small things as well, there were still expressions of goodwill. The Japanese government allowed the British embassy in Tokyo to import substantial quantities of normally unauthorized items for sale as part of a fundraising effort on behalf of the British Red Cross. Many Japanese attended the fair, which was held in the British embassy compound, and the bazaar raised more than one thousand pounds in three hours. Even at the worst of times the Japanese people could be surprising.

Throughout this period, Ethel and Hans coped as best they could and lived their lives as normally as possible. Ethel had developed an interest in quilting and spent many happy evenings at her work. There was something restorative about the creative orderliness of a quilt. She also liked chatting to other quilters, and one of the main subjects of conversation was the increasing unreliability of servants. Even the faithful Kiku-san had begun taking holidays at short notice and being absent far more than before. Ethel's main concern, though, was about her remaining eye, but she preferred not to talk about it except with Hans. The slightest degree of redness or irritation could set off a frantic exchange of telegrams with Dr Vogt in Zurich, and fear of blindness always lurked in the background. Ethel did not think that she could bear to go back to Zurich or New York on her own with Roni. The terrifying spectre of sightlessness caused them both many sleepless nights.

There were marvellous moments, too. Both Ethel and Hans were captivated one night at the boat club by a magnificent full moon rising over the rippling Pacific, an exotic, minimalist, mystical Oriental scene right out of one of the Japanese drawings they had begun to collect. Such moments are for a lifetime. Hans still had a terrific sense of humour and they had some good laughs. Once in a while they spoke German together, which usually had them in stitches. Ethel got a kick out of telling her fellow quilters one day about Roni throwing the water polo ball into the sea at the boat club, leaving a pool full of annoyed men who were not sure what to do next. Perhaps Roni was trying to rid himself of a bad case of worms (not the silk-making kind), but fortunately Dr Paravicini was able to procure the requisite product to deal with this common problem and the little boy continued to thrive.

In mid-June Italy entered the war, to nobody's surprise on the side of the Germans. Mussolini saw how badly things were going for Italy's erstwhile ally, France, decided which way the wind was blowing, and cast his country's lot with what he was certain would be the winning side. After that, it did not take long for supplies of decent pasta to disappear from the shelves. Flour was of poorer and poorer quality, too, and no one was quite sure where it came from. Even rice, the Japanese staff of life, was becoming scarce, and on 2 August quotas were imposed on the sale of bread.

In Europe the "phony war" finally came to an end when Germany invaded Norway, and then Belgium in spring 1940, but it brought no perceptible change in the Far East, and Japan still seemed far from the conflict. The British embassy published daily bulletins to give the "true" story of what was going on and to overcome misconceptions sown by Japanese propaganda. A few read these courageous bulletins, but many expatriates preferred not to be too well informed, probably finding ignorance less stressful on a daily basis.

Then came the astonishing setback of France's capitulation to the invading German armies on 17 June 1940. The Japanese never censored triumphant news such as this, and it cast a pall over the whole foreign community. Hans's French friend from his early days in Japan, André Humbert, who had an office above Hans's, came down one morning during the summer with a briefcase full of papers and asked if it could be kept for him in the company safe. Hans innocently obliged, and the very next morning the *Kempeitai* showed up and led poor André away to jail, where the secret police kept him until the war was over. He was accused of being a Gaullist, and the Germans were certainly behind his denunciation. Hans kept the safe locked tight and began sending his friend French books to help him pass the time. Although the books were carefully screened and sometimes censored by the Japanese jailers, they never caused Hans any trouble and were always returned eventually. André Humbert turned out to be one of the lucky ones. Hans learned from Max Pestalozzi after the war that André had survived his five years of Japanese imprisonment and was safely living in Paris with his family. The mysterious files remained in the company safe until war's end, and by the time they were read (if indeed they ever *were* read), none of it made any difference anymore.

From 1936 onwards until the fall of France, opposing forces within the Japanese government had maintained a constant tug of war, with neither side managing definitively to gain the upper hand. The moderating forces of peace and reconciliation won some decisions, while others were carried by the war-mongering expansionists, who wanted to see Japan take what they saw as her rightful pre-eminent place on the world stage. Neither side as yet clearly dominated, although the advent of the Yonai cabinet in January 1940 suggested for a hopeful six-month interval that the moderates might actually win the day. But France's early surrender to the apparently invincible Germans – the Huns, as the expatriates were starting to call them again – gave pause even to the moderates, and government transcripts that were made public after the war reveal that July 1940 was the turning point, the moment when Emperor Hirohito's Land of the Rising Sun determined to set course for war.

Hitler was quick to perceive the doubt produced in Japan by the fall of France. He resolved to take advantage of the next moment of political instability to court a powerful ally in the Far East. The chance came when yet another new cabinet took over in Japan in the early fall of 1940, no longer under the moderate Admiral Yonai. Hitler delegated Herr Stahmer, a high official of the Berlin Foreign Office, to visit Tokyo with a secret draft of a tripartite treaty associating Japan with Germany and Italy. The Japanese negotiators demanded some tactical modifications to their benefit, but for the most part Stahmer – who was to succeed vonDirksen as German ambassador to Japan during the war – was successful in his guileful mission. On 29 September 1940 the Japanese press announced to a surprised populace that the emperor's government was now committed to an alliance with the Axis.

Less than a week after France's fall, Ethel's obstetrician, Dr Coolican, and his family left for Australia. Because of restrictions on navigation that were already in force, the family had to travel the long way around, via America. Dr Coolican had brought Roni into the world and his departure on 22 June aboard the SS *President Coolidge* left another void in Yokohama, a sad one for Ethel. Coolican had six children to support, though, and the diminishing numbers of foreign clients were making a serious dent in his income. The Irish physician knew that there would be lots of babies to deliver. Fortunately for the Baenningers, Hans's respected friend Dr Paravicini had no intention of leaving Japan at his advanced age, and so they did not have to worry too much about medical care.

As mounting numbers of foreigners headed out, leaving fewer and fewer homes to visit, the boat club increasingly became the venue where expatriates who had remained in Japan met. Ethel went almost every afternoon, often meeting Vi or other girlfriends for tea. Boredom and worry took their toll, and seeing friends at least once a day helped to fight the constant feeling of threat and restore morale. Roni also liked to be around other people, and he especially loved playing with John Bjergfeldt, a little boy of about

Roni's age who lived next door with his Danish parents. Foreigners who had never been particularly close suddenly grew friendlier and more sympathetic to each other, and this pulling together was one bright upshot of the otherwise grim circumstances that were its cause.

Early in 1940 the Imperial Japanese Navy had decided that the old Yokohama Yacht Club was too close to the Yokosuka naval base and had to be moved. As an alternative, the City of Yokohama made available a piece of land much closer to town than the old club and right at the water's edge. The British Chartered Bank advanced money for new facilities and a new clubhouse, accepting the signatures of the boat club's established members as the only collateral. It was a peculiar and generous financial deal strictly based on the bank's goodwill, with no time limit for repayment. So a new clubhouse was built, and although club activities were upset for several months, the members of the boat club ended up with a much nicer place, with a fine view of Yokohama Harbour. The British Chartered Bank had underwritten a similar arrangement for the building of the new International Hospital on the Bluff (where Roni had been born), and all the foreigners were very thankful. It was hoped that the bank's decency in agreeing to overlook the bottom line during these trying years would in time be rewarded.

The high-handed order to vacate the old boat club, with no offer of compensation, turned out to be a blessing in disguise, or so the members were able to convince themselves. The new club had a swimming pool, and the greater proximity to town proved a particular boon. It was getting more and more difficult to find taxis on account of gas shortages, but while the new club was still a fair walk from their house on the Bluff, Ethel and Roni seemed to be able to handle it. They chatted away and had fun on their walks together, and the club provided a good destination where you could always find the companionship of friends.

Hans was very active during this time as an officer on the executive committee of the boat club and was obliged to participate in the wrangling over land rights, compensation, etc. – often using his fluent Japanese. These negotiations with the authorities were in fact very one-sided and the Japanese never returned the good-will expressed by the club members. What is amazing to see in the minutes of the long and frustrating boat club meetings was the members' naïve, stubborn belief that nothing was terribly amiss and that solutions to every problem would be found. There was a failure to grasp the gravity of the overall situation and a desperate intent on the part of the club's negotiators to believe in the inherent goodwill of the other party. This was of course a conviction without basis; their good faith was despised and even cynically used by the Japanese to weaken the position of the foreigners. It was a sad chapter.

On 29 September Ethel took Roni to Sunday school for the first time. She was taken aback at the poor turnout but realized that ungodliness was not the issue. Rather, the few children in the classroom with Roni brought home to her that there were simply fewer and fewer foreign parents and children left. It occurred to Ethel that the people who remained, like her and Hans, began to seem almost like survivors. A spirit of solidarity ran through it all – a sort of circling of the wagons – but it was not a lot of fun. Everyone desperately wished that things could somehow return to normal. Listening to the children sing "Jesus Loves Me, This I Know" made Ethel quite emotional, and she prayed that someone was watching over them during those difficult and shaky times.

At home, during the week, Roni often delivered a rousing, high-pitched rendition of the old World War I favourite "Pack Up Your Troubles in Your Old Kit Bag." This always lifted Ethel's spirits, whether Jesus loved them or not, and was probably the best thing any of them could do for the time being, while they waited to see what would happen. For surely something would.

CHAPTER NINE

Apart or Together? — 1941

By October 1940 nothing yet had really "happened," but the Standard Oil Company nevertheless ordered women employees and employee dependents of its Far Eastern operations to return home by the end of the year. Towards the end of that month, the British embassy took the same decision and advised British women to return home with their children. Vi Woodbridge, Ethel's first friend in Japan, her roommate, bridesmaid, and erstwhile chaperone, chose to heed that advice and leave. Her employer, Standard Oil, paid her fare, as well as the fares of all its departing employees. The Baenningers saw Vi off when she sailed for Vancouver on the *Empress of Canada* on the last day of 1940 and then took a taxi to the boat club for a New Year's Eve party. But they were not really in the mood for a party. Vi's departure left them desolate. The foreign community was beginning to seem more like a skeleton crew. As 1941 dawned things seemed to be coming to a head, and the seriousness of the situation could no longer be ignored.

Although there were no bomber attacks as yet, the air-raid drills that the Japanese had begun on 1 October gradually became more frequent. As well as being a safety precaution, the drills steered the civilian population's attention toward an external aggressor, their common enemy. As a form of propaganda, it made a great deal of sense from the viewpoint of the Japanese military. The sirens and filing into shelters distracted people's attention from the increasing privations at home. Newspapers decried the wickedness of America and its opposition to Japan's conquest of Manchuria and aggression toward China. Such distorted information fuelled public ill feeling against a world that was cast as squeezing Japan and restraining her grandiose plans for the Far East. Military music could be heard in the streets, soldiers were more in evidence, and Japan's flag, a red circle on a white field symbolic of the rising sun, was everywhere. The increased activity of military aircraft was very obvious in those days when civilian air traffic was virtually nonexistent.

In spite of the gathering wave of feeling against foreigners, Hans and Ethel's Japanese servants remained dedicated and loyal, as though nothing had changed. Kiku-san, the cook, had been with them for several years. Their maid Arai-san had come to them more recently to replace Kiyo-san, who had tearfully resigned to marry her beau of long standing. Both Japanese women worked hard and were devoted to their employers. They were especially fond of the three-year-old "boy-chan," and Roni enjoyed being with them and loved to help in the kitchen. He was particularly good at sitting on the kitchen floor and licking out the mixing bowl after the cake batter was poured. Some of his happiest early memories are from those days when his mother and Kiku-san were working contentedly together in the kitchen. The cook was so patient with Mummy's halting efforts at Japanese and Roni was greatly entertained by her use of hands and gestures to fill in the blanks. He could tell from Kiku-san's shy giggling that she shared his hilarity at Ethel's carryings on, and it all made for good-natured fun.

Ever since the loss of her eye had brought about such unwonted changes in her life, the servants were an even greater help to Ethel. They took over all the homemaking duties that were so difficult for someone with impaired depth perception. Nevertheless, for Ethel the most difficult thing about servants, even after nine years, continued to be the fact of having them in the same house all the time, and the need to remember that they were there and govern one's tongue accordingly. And one's singing. In late 1940, having learned a song called "There'll Always Be an England" from one of the British expats at the club, Roni marched around singing it with great fervour at the top of his voice. The Japanese loved children, but singing patriotic songs glorifying one of their emerging enemies suddenly began to take on altered overtones in a country heading toward war. The servants were real friends in many ways, but it had to be remembered that they owed other loyalties too. Kiku-san seldom spoke of her family, even when she and Ethel were working together in the kitchen. Like many Japanese servants she sometimes became confused about which rules of etiquette to use to suit the situation at hand. She was older than either of the *geijin* but they were her employers, so she was both higher and lower in status – at least according to Japanese rules. But there was no mistaking the pride in her voice when she spoke of her son.

One day, Kiku-san's son Buntaro came to visit. He cut a very impressive figure. Kiku-san had rarely been so bubbly with Ethel, nor so forward and personal with Hans. Buntaro really was a dashing young man, standing erect in his dress uniform, the summer whites of an officer in the imperial navy. There was gold braid on his pressed cuffs and at his collar, and at his waist a gleaming sword in its scabbard. He held his peaked cap politely in his hand as he bowed to them. The bow was formal but not deferential, not like his mother's bows to the oku-san and her husband.

Hans and Ethel's Japanese was better than Buntaro's English, so it was in his language that they spoke. After Hans's polite greetings and expressions of welcome, Buntaro explained that he had stopped by to say goodbye to his mother before his ship left port and began preparing for war. He was convinced that war was the solution to the arrogance, as he saw it, of the Americans and the British. He was particularly bitter about the Americans. His first official voyage after becoming a senior officer was a courtesy visit to the United States. Walking about San Francisco and San

Diego, he had seen many signs that said "No Orientals." Japanese in California were relegated to being gardeners or landscapers, and even those who had become American citizens, the Japanese-Americans, were not fully accepted as the equal of white citizens. Even the Germans were accepted because they were not Oriental. Buntaro declared that the Japanese could not be considered "Oriental" in the same way the Koreans and Chinese were. The ignorance of Americans and their treatment of Japanese in their country had been very hurtful.

Fortunately Kiku-san came in with Arai-san and Roni. Buntaro and the little boy took to each other at once. Roni was very much in awe of the young naval officer and spent the rest of the day talking about his new Japanese hero. But the young officer continued to be more circumspect with Roni's Dad, although Hans's Swiss neutrality and ability to speak Japanese certainly helped break the ice. For his part, Hans could not help thinking that Americans were not the only arrogant racists. And they were not as warlike as this young Japanese, who could not wait for the chance to kill Americans. If they were all like him a war did not seem so far-fetched. Hans and Ethel both felt gloomy for the rest of the day and had trouble getting to sleep that night.

Shortages of foodstuffs, medical supplies, and household goods like soap and toilet paper were becoming increasingly irksome. The pharmacist told Hans that painkillers, sleeping pills and even cough medicine and aspirin would soon be unobtainable because they were reserved for the Japanese army in China. In view of increasing privations of this kind and the many uncertainties they faced, Ethel and Hans took the painful decision in December 1940 that she and Roni should try to go home to Canada and stay there until further notice. It was simply becoming too dangerous to stay. Hans also felt that it would be easier for him to cope on his own, unburdened by family cares and knowing at least that his wife and son were safe. On the other hand, there remained the frightful spectre of full-fledged war breaking out while the family was separated, forcing them to remain on opposite sides of the world, perhaps for years. What if they made the wrong choice? It was a dilemma that they shared with millions of others around the world. They were beginning to hear stories that Jews in Poland and other Nazi-dominated parts of Europe no longer had a choice and were trapped. Just after New Year's Day and without consulting Ethel further lest she change her mind, Hans went down to the shipping company and bought two tickets to Seattle for Ethel and Roni.

On 31 January 1941 they departed on the SS *Heian Maru*, a small Japanese liner. Once again Ethel was asked by friends to smuggle various things out of Japan. Their Swiss friend Oskar Abegg offered to pay her fifteen hundred dollars if she would take five thousand dollars of his money and deposit the notes in his bank account in New York. The amount just about covered the travel expenses for Ethel and Roni, and since money was getting tight they agreed, with misgivings, to take the risk. Fortunately, on the day of departure the Japanese were not very concerned about searching the luggage of a young Swiss woman and her toddler-son, so she could continue to play international courier for her friends.

Aunt Mima and Uncle Reuben met Ethel and Roni at the train station in Vancouver when they arrived from Seattle. They drove them around the city, with its spectacular geography between sea and mountains. They were very taken with Roni and sad when it came time to put the travellers on the train for the twelve-hundred-mile journey to Regina. Ethel's eye problems, perhaps because of all the travel and stress, had reappeared and she was in considerable pain. She had to travel on almost immediately to see a specialist in Toronto. Vi Woodbridge had lost no time getting re-established in Canada after her years in Japan, and she went with Ethel to Toronto and then accompanied her to New York for more consultations with ophthalmologists. But no one could help her. Roni was confused by it all, but fortunately his grandparents were warm, caring people who were delighted to look after the little globetrotter while his mother was away. The specialist Ethel saw in Toronto said the condition of her eye was unstable and that she should have it out, but this still-lovely young woman's physical vanity had already been devastated enough in the past three years and she chose to ignore the doctor's advice.

Not long after her return to Regina, however, following these costly, fruitless, and exhausting trips, Ethel awoke on 6 June 1941 to discover that her right eye had "exploded," become totally hard – like a small stone – and was finished for good. She thus had to re-enter hospital to have the eye removed. After many further examinations and "fittings," she acquired a glass eye a month later. This required an additional hospital stay in Regina. Hans was frantic to be on the other side of the Pacific, unable to be beside his wife at such a critical juncture for her well-being, but he was at least glad that she was in Canada where her ordeal was not made worse by shortages of medical supplies. For Ethel, it was difficult to see a bright side to any of it. Desolate and so far from her husband who could have comforted her, she could only gaze at her lifeless artificial eye in the mirror and weep for her lost beauty and for life's random cruelty.

Meanwhile the geopolitical situation was becoming worse. Tensions mounted inexorably and the propaganda in the Japanese newspapers, which by now Hans almost regretted being able to read, made clear the ominous direction in which things were heading. The militarists and warmongers seemed to have won the day. In July 1941, as a result of Japan's occupation of southern Indo-China, the United States, followed by Britain and her dominions, stopped all financial transactions with Japan and declared an economic embargo. This further shifted the political equilibrium. Shipments of essential materials like oil and scrap iron were stopped by means of a blockade. This was a catastrophe for the Japanese, whose homeland was poor in raw materials and resources and who were very dependent on the import of basic resources and sources of energy. Prince Fumimaro Konoye, the prime minister, secretly tried to arrange a personal meeting with US President Franklin Roosevelt to negotiate some sort of compromise, but he was rebuffed. The Americans stipulated that unless Japan revised her position on China and gave up all sources of raw materials that she had seized there, Roosevelt would not agree to meet. Factions opposed to compromise leaked Konoye's request and its rejection to the press, and this further affronted Japanese dignity and fuelled nationalist outrage.

Strange things began to happen that had never happened before. Fifteen British residents were arrested on trumped-up charges of espionage and much was made of it in the Japanese press. Almost certainly anti-British political elements within the secret police engineered the arrests, but initially the government stood behind them. The incident was ultimately defused by diplomatic efforts and the central government disowned responsibility, but not before the Reuters correspondent in Tokyo, Melville Cox – one of those who had been arrested – mysteriously died during interrogation by the *Kempeitai*. His fourteen codefendants were deported.

It subsequently emerged that Mr Cox had, in fact, leapt to his death from a window at the police station in the course of his questioning. His friends knew that he was not a spy, and they also knew that he was a gentle man with a low-key, phlegmatic disposition. That someone with such sang-froid would behave in this way said all that was needed concerning the way the Japanese were beginning to treat foreigners, and these events cast a pall over the whole foreign community. Cox became something of a martyred hero. Fearing reprisals against his wife by the same nationalistic elements in the police who had undoubtedly caused her husband's death, the British embassy quickly arranged for her removal and she sailed some weeks later for Canada.

Another incident involving the wife of a French official and her daughter took place at a cinema one busy afternoon. The theatre was crowded and when the two ladies refused to yield their seats to two young Japanese toughs who indicated they wanted them, the two men sat down in the ladies' laps. The furious French-women made a considerable ruckus and a policeman was called.

The officer of the law promptly ejected the two foreigners from the cinema. When interrogated in the lobby by the policeman and the manager, the French lady had the great presence of mind to pretend, in high dudgeon, that she was the wife of an official at the German embassy and that those who had offended her and her daughter could expect the worst of consequences when she reported her story. This did the trick. The manager of the cinema apologized and the policeman was all of a sudden nowhere to be seen. Such events were widely recounted and gradually embellished at cocktail receptions and dinner parties in the foreign community and contributed greatly to the growing sense of unease. The average Japanese man or woman in the street was increasingly influenced by the rabid and unrelenting antiforeign propaganda, and of course in the Orient outsiders are easily recognizable. It was not pleasant.

Russia had always been the primary "Western" enemy for Japan, partly owing to her proximity. The militarist elements of the Japanese government had thus been horrified – and come close to being toppled – when their German fascist ally, without any consultation or warning, had concluded the German-Soviet Non-Aggression Pact of August 1939. There was great relief in Japan when Hitler launched Operation Barbarossa, the German assault on the Soviet Union that began from the west in June 1941. But the Japanese, like many others, found it difficult to comprehend how an ally could reverse policy so suddenly, without any advance notification. In any event, it began to seem to Hans that Japan might attack the Soviet Union from the east. As became clear after the war, however, the Soviets already knew this would not happen, thanks to Richard Sorge, the Russian spy in place in Japan. Consequently, the Soviets were able to move desperately needed armies west where they could face Nazi Germany. Japan, as Sorge had found out, was much more interested in expanding her empire in the Pacific and withdrew most of her forces from Manchuria. But as he pondered the possibilities and conflicting theories, Hans was not certain about anything. Sitting in their

Ethel and Roni out for a walk in Vancouver in 1941.

silent house in Yokohama, he felt desperate about his faraway wife and little boy, and he was totally at a loss about what he should do.

What they feared most was that war would indeed break out in the Pacific and that the family would be sundered for an indefinite period. Hans gradually concluded that, in the short term, Japan did not seem to want war with the Soviet Union after all – nor with the United States; he therefore was able to talk himself into deciding that the situation was safe enough to risk the return of Ethel and Roni from Canada. The two had been gone for almost

Ethel and Roni (second row, third and fourth from left) with ship's company aboard *Hikawa Maru* on its return to Japan and "going in the wrong" direction in 1941.

half a year and they were all fed up. It was time for the family to get back together again.

So a mere six months after they had left, and following an agitated exchange of telegrams, Ethel and Roni travelled to Vancouver. No ships were available from there and so they took the train south to Seattle, where they began the long wait for a passage back to Japan. "What do you want to go *there* for?" they were repeatedly asked by the other lodgers in the gloomy tourist cabins where they were living in Seattle. It was a good question, to which

Roni had a good answer: "I want to see my Daddy." It was October before they were able to get a cabin on what was to be the very last ship returning to Japan from the North American West Coast, although they did not know that when the booking was made.

The SS *Hikawa Maru* was full of Japanese returning home on the advice of their government. A long-time friend of Ethel's, a British woman named Teddy Longy, and her little daughter Pauline were the only other non-Japanese passengers. They were going "home" to Japan to be with her French husband, and their Japanese shipmates kept telling the two women with their four-year-old children how brave they were. Everyone on board had heaps of luggage containing all manner of nonperishable food that would last for a long time no matter what happened. Ethel had received a telegram from Hans in June, while she was still in Richardson, which read, "Please bring plenty of all essentials like milk beef extract olive oil flour sugar cereals corned beef coffee Baenninger"; so she too was carrying as much as she could to make it though the lean times that everyone knew lay ahead.

By this time, regular shipping lines had almost ceased to function. There were many British left in Japan who had not heeded their country's earlier warnings and now found themselves stuck. Despite Japan's frozen assets abroad and the bad feeling caused by the economic boycott, the British embassy was able to organize a special evacuation ship, and the SS *Anhui* sailed from Japan in mid-September 1941, filled to overflowing with British men and women who had waited until the last minute to get out. Geography made evacuation somewhat easier for the Americans, and by the end of that summer most of the families of United States embassy staff had also gone home. British embassy staff and their dependents stayed on for the time being, postponing their longer and more dangerous journey home.

Sailing bravely in the opposite direction, firmly against the prevailing currents, Ethel and her son finally arrived back in Yokohama, once again on Roni's birthday – this time his fourth. After a ten-month separation, it was a happy reunion for all three of them. Now that they were together again there seemed no doubt they had done the right thing, despite the dangers of their situation. By the late fall of 1941 commercial shipping had come to a virtual standstill. Ethel and Roni had just made it. Mail and business connections with the rest of the world had ceased and neither Ethel nor Hans could look forward any longer to the pleasure of letters from home. The foreign community in Japan was now cut off from the outside world. Hans's company's home office in Switzerland, like other firms based in neutral countries, remained more sanguine about the situation in Japan than their Allied competitors and did not believe that evacuation of their employees or their dependents was essential. Nonetheless, Charles Rudolph and Co. had made known its decision to pay its senior employees half their salaries if war broke out and for as long as it lasted, even though there would be essentially nothing for any of them to do. This generosity was more than ample compensation for the home leave that Hans had had to forego when Charles Rudolph took over Nabholz and Co. way back in 1930 and Hans was grateful. It was a remarkably big-hearted policy and removed a tremendous source of worry for the Baenningers and many other loyal members of staff and their families as they gazed into an uncertain future.

CHAPTER TEN

Pearl Harbor and the World at War – 1941, 1942

At 7:45 A.M. on Monday, 8 December 1941 (7 December, on the other side of the International Date Line), Britain's ambassador to Japan, the Right Honourable Sir Robert Craigie, received a telephone message requesting that he call on the foreign minister of Japan fifteen minutes later, at eight o'clock. Sir Robert had to hurry. Mr Togo, the minister, together with his private secretary and interpreter, Mr Kasé, explained to His Majesty's envoy when he arrived that they had just completed a meeting with the Honourable Joseph Grew, America's ambassador to Japan, informing the United States that Japan had decided to break off the talks that had been going on for some months in Washington, talks that aimed at defusing the increasingly portentous stand-off between Japan and the West. Mr Togo embarked on a long, rambling justification of Japan's decision, expressing regret that things should have come to this point. He added that he appreciated all that Sir Robert had tried to do for Anglo-Japanese relations during the past four years. At no time was war mentioned.

Sir Robert was driven back to the embassy in the embassy's black Rolls-Royce, Union Jack flying on the front left fender, to learn from his wife, who had heard it on the radio, that Japan had commenced warlike operations against the United States and Britain. Five minutes later, at 8:30 A.M., the telephone wires at the British embassy were cut, just thirty minutes after Sir Robert's cool but cordial meeting with Mr Togo at the Ministry for Foreign Affairs. Sir Robert immediately left for the American embassy to consult with his colleague, Mr Grew. The British diplomat had only been in Japan for four years, but the American ambassador had occupied that difficult post since 1932 and had become a seasoned expert in "reading" the Japanese. It was absolutely necessary to compare notes at this time of crisis, and there was no attempt by the Japanese to impede Craigie's departure when he left the British embassy.

While the two ambassadors were conferring at the US Embassy, a message came from the Ministry for Foreign Affairs conveying Japan's declaration of war against the United States. Sir Robert immediately excused himself, and when he got back to his embassy again, Japanese police surrounded the compound and firmly closed and locked the gates once the ambassador's limousine had entered the grounds. A representative from the Ministry for Foreign Affairs who was waiting for Ambassador Craigie politely communicated Japan's declaration of war on Great Britain as well, hence on all her dominions, including Canada. If only in view of what he lived through that morning, it is not surprising that the book Sir Robert wrote in 1945 about his five-year posting in Japan was called *Behind the Japanese Mask*.

Hans had breakfast as usual on that morning of 8 December and walked in the cool winter air to his office. Radios were blaring. Voices of announcers dominated the racket, and music seemed to be limited to military marches. Now and then he could make out the word *geijin*, foreigners. Something had happened. The Japanese were noticeably silent as Hans walked by in the street. Nobody knew who shared their views of the nation's new course. In perilous times it is better to keep one's mouth shut.

The murmured greetings of nearly a hundred Japanese employees were accompanied by formal bows, as usual, when Hans walked into the office at about nine o'clock, but the atmosphere seemed charged. It was not until he had tuned in the radio near his desk that he heard about the Japanese attack on Pearl Harbor. Radio Tokyo was delirious, feverishly reporting that the American fleet anchored in Hawaii had been completely destroyed. Scariest of all were the announcements that all enemy nationals in Japan were to be rounded up immediately and placed in internment camps. Hans thought of his wife and son at home alone on the Bluff. Who did the Japanese consider "enemy" nationals? He was very relieved by a later clarification that neutral foreigners, like Danes, Swedes, Swiss, etc., were to be left alone. Thank goodness Ethel had married him and gone to all that trouble to get her Swiss passport. Roni was automatically Swiss thanks to his Swiss father. At least his family was safe.

It was impossible to get much done that day so Hans let the staff go at noon. He stayed at the office for a while longer, thinking about the implications of Japan's attack on the United States. It seemed insane, totally out of character for the Japanese that he knew, decent people like his staff, and the shopkeepers, craftsmen, and businessmen in the silk world. But the xenophobic, suicidal, hysterical military clique was another matter, and its members seemed to be the ones in charge now.

The Americans and British were in the majority among the foreigners in Japan, but they were now to be interned in concentration camps. That meant a lot of foreign organizations would suddenly be left without leaders. Hans knew the Swiss were among the logical choices to replace them, neutrals whom both sides felt they could trust. Hans had always pulled his weight in the foreign community, and now he was one of only a few remaining Swiss. He was already on the board of the new Yokohama General Hospital, where Roni had entered the world four years ago. He was also a founder and still on the board of the Yokohama Civic and Athletic Club. There was also the Yokohama United Club, one of the major clubs that nearly all of the foreign men belonged to. It was a very traditional, conservative institution that women were never permitted to enter under any circumstances. Hans happened to know they had replenished their stock of fine Scotch whisky recently. Well, if he was going to be called upon to be the interim president it was his duty to protect these precious stores from the hordes of militaristic Japanese. So on his way home, on Pearl Harbor Day, he stopped at the club and liberated a couple of bottles of the very best Scotch. He and Ethel drank a heartfelt toast to the many fallen Americans when he got home.

Everybody seemed crabby that day. After his father went to work there was usually a quiet time when his mother would read to Roni. They were in that part of *The Wind in the Willows* where Mole becomes lost in the Wild Wood and all the menacing little voices start to surround him, but he can't ever really see who is chasing him in the snowy darkness. It's a scary bit, and Roni wanted to get quickly to the comforting part where Mole stumbles onto Badger's front door. His old friend Badger brings Mole into the cozy warmth underground, where a stout door stands between him and the outside world and the frightening voices. Fragrant smoked hams hang from the rafters; there is a fire in the hearth and flickering candles, and an old friend to lend Mole slippers. It did not seem cozy in the Baenninger house because the radio was making a big noise out in the kitchen for most of the morning. Roni could not understand why his mother did not tell Kiku-san to turn down the volume. The radio announcers seemed very excited about something – they were almost screaming and it made everybody feel upset. The little four-year-old could tell that his mother was worried about something as she read to him, but she wouldn't tell him what it was.

As on most other days, Ethel had to go shopping for food, on the off chance that there would be something to buy like a piece of pork – if there were enough ration coupons – or a piece of fish or some fresh vegetables, or even fruit. December was not a good time for fresh fruit and vegetables and there usually wasn't much to buy besides turnips, cabbage, or potatoes. Roni became quite tired of dried apples, although he was lucky to get them, his mother said, adding that he should be grateful because they were hard to find.

Returning from an unsuccessful search of the shops, Ethel and her son found one of Roni's favourite Japanese people waiting in the living room. Mr Yokawa, Hans's "banto" (or number two man) at the office, was sitting, looking around him in an embarrassed way. He bowed to Ethel and tousled Roni's hair in that way grown-ups do when they can't think of anything to say. Ethel shooed her son off to his room for a nap. He found out after that Mr Yokawa's country was now at war with his mother's, where Uncle Harvey, her seventeen-year-old younger brother, was already joining the Royal Air Force to fly missions against the Japanese in Southeast Asia. And this kindly Japanese man whom Roni always liked a lot had come to offer his mother his protection or assistance in the event that anything should happen to his father, who was obviously much admired by the people who worked for him. If only all Japanese could be as nice as Mr Yokawa. His father came home from work early that day because he said there really was nothing to do there. Roni couldn't sleep and he heard his parents talking long into the night.

The boat club, scene of so many happy occasions in the life of the expatriate community, had been boarded up some months earlier and the Japanese now requisitioned it. As soon as war was declared, the boat club became a holding area for "enemy nationals" and Hans and Ethel's unfortunate English, Canadian, and Australian friends were rounded up and incarcerated there, prisoners rather than members who could come and go as they pleased. As for the Americans, those not imprisoned in their embassy's compound were all put behind barbed wire at the Yokohama Race Course. Hans and Ethel felt a curious mixture of emotion in the face of these brutal measures: sorrow for their friends, on the one hand, who just happened to carry the wrong passport – as Ethel had herself not long ago. On the other hand, there was guilty relief at their own good fortune. They had "won the lottery" and could go on living more or less normally with their son.

At that point, Hans's old friend Dr Paravicini came through for the Baenningers again, as he had so often in the past (and would continue to do in the future). Dr Fridolin Paravacini was in his late sixties, a refined and distinguished Swiss gentleman. Hans had come to know him through the Bänningers' family doctor in Switzerland, who had been a classmate of Dr Paravicini's at medical school in Zurich. Dr Paravicini had served as chief delegate for the International Red Cross in Japan during World War I and had subsequently retired. His curious first name was taken from a character in Swiss mythology, and because he made no secret of wishing he had been named otherwise most people, including Hans and Ethel, addressed him either as Dr Paravicini or, on more intimate occasions, as "Para." At the sudden outbreak of war in 1941, when Red Cross headquarters in Geneva approached him, Para reluctantly agreed to resume his duties as chief delegate in Japan. He immediately took steps to have Hans, his young protégé and a fellow Swiss, appointed as his assistant. Aside from minor diplomatic status, this also ensured a regular "special distribution" food supply for the Baenninger family. The orderly Japanese, so often reviled as savage in their conduct during the war, were punctilious in honouring small international obligations of this kind. As a result Hans, Ethel, and Roni went on obtaining staple foods that gradually became scarcer for everyone else.

All foreigners were required to wear lapel pins bearing their country's flag so that they could be identified. The Swiss pin was a modest little enamelled replica of the white cross on a red field. The Red Cross insignia was in fact the reverse of this in honour of the Swiss, Henri Dunant, who founded the organization in Geneva in 1863. Germans flaunted a large swastika on their oversized pins, and it was obvious to Ethel and even to Roni that many of them were throwing their weight around in shops, marching to the front of the queues of patient Japanese and foreigners who lacked privileged status. There were others, though, like the Erklenz family who lived next door, who waited in line even if they really were Nazis.

Food became scarcer but was still to be found. The Baenningers were able to throw a Christmas party in 1941 for the much-diminished number of their friends who were not interned. A combination of the special Red Cross distribution, the food brought back from Canada by Ethel, and a little present here and there made this treat possible. Their last party in Japan was probably the most appreciated of any they ever gave. Ron, more than sixty years later, remembers it as a rather forlorn little gathering at which Christmas presents for the kids, even paltry ones, were in very short supply. One had to make do, of course. In February 1942, the family's ration of meat (about a pound of pork for the month) had a noticeably fishy taste. Not very appealing, but it was all there was. It was not starvation, and compared to the hardships endured by so many others in those dark days it was not so bad. Things were going to get a lot worse.

In the early phases of the war events were going Japan's way. After a fierce battle early in 1942, the Japanese were victorious at Wake Island, taking about eight hundred American prisoners, many of them wounded. The Japanese war department correctly sent these prisoners' names to the Red Cross so that they could be transmitted to the International Red Cross headquarters in Geneva, as required by international rules of warfare. The ICRC then transmitted the names to Washington so that relatives could be notified. Hans's first official job in his new role with the Red Cross was to decipher all the Japanese lists of American names, and it turned out to be unexpectedly difficult. Japanese soldiers and officers who knew little or no English interviewed each American prisoner, who gave their name, rank, and serial number. The Japanese would listen to the Americans and then write, in characters, each name as it sounded to them. The war ministry sent these lists to Hans, who transcribed the Japanese approximations into English syllables as best he could. With a lot of help from Ethel he then made guesses about what the names and American hometowns of the soldiers might be. Thus, for example, Hans would transcribe ト ム リ ヌ ソ ヌ as TO MU RI NU SO NU. Ethel would then guess that the name was TOMLINSON.

It took a week of intensive effort to get through all eight hundred names, and despite their sincere best efforts Hans and Ethel surely made a lot of wrong guesses. Each day's output was drafted as a separate telegram, typed in capital letters, and then taken by a Red Cross messenger to the Japanese telegraph office for transmission to Geneva. Eventually, relatives in the US received word, although there must have been many who never heard. Others were probably told about servicemen and women who were not actually imprisoned but whose names were similar to someone who was. As usual in wartime, there were a lot of snafus – situation normal: all fouled up.

The Japanese media could barely keep up with the country's military successes during the war's first months. The fall of Singapore was an especially black day for everyone in the foreign community. But in June 1942, during the Battle of Midway, the American forces sank the four principal aircraft carriers of the Japanese navy literally within five minutes, off Midway Island. This first major defeat was not revealed to Japanese civilians until after the war had ended. Indeed, Midway was probably the turning point of the war, but no one in Japan knew anything about it at the time – except for the military, of course, who kept it to themselves.

Freedom to suppress negative news events is a very big advantage of totalitarian governments during wartime. Hans and Ethel, like most foreigners, remained inwardly certain that Japan did not have a chance in the long run against the combined might of the United States and their allies. But the news broadcasts and Japanese propaganda painted a bleak picture filled with big talk and American and British defeats, and they had to hold their tongues except in the privacy of their home. Like all foreigners who had not been interned, they were under twenty-four-hour surveillance "for their protection," with a policeman standing guard around the clock in a little shelter just at the edge of their garden. Roni always managed to make friends with the young Japanese sentries, much to Ethel's consternation. To her they were The Enemy; they stood at attention in a most menacing manner and the rifles they carried were tipped with bayonets suitable for skewering four-year-olds. But to her son they just seemed like friendly older kids that he could play with. Japanese schoolboys often wore uniforms too, and Roni used to ride his tricycle to the guardhouse every day for a congenial visit with the enemy.

Then the Americans struck back. Only four months after Pearl Harbor, on 18 April 1942, Commander Jimmy Doolittle led a daring air raid on Tokyo. The roar of the big black low-flying bombers woke Roni from his afternoon nap. Arai-san and Kiku-san both dashed up to his bedroom to reassure him, but Ron could tell that they were the ones in need of reassurance. The little boy thought it was pretty exciting, but the servants were truly terrified. The myth of Japanese invincibility had been shattered by those few overloaded B-25s lumbering over Yokohama on the way to Tokyo. Their sudden appearance could not be hidden by misinformation or propaganda. Roni's mother did her best to comfort the servants. His dad had been in Tokyo for a business meeting that day, and everyone was relieved when he finally walked up the path before supper. He had seen little evidence of physical destruction, but having American bombers overhead was intoxicating for foreigners – and devastating to Japanese civilians. The mental and emotional damage they sustained could never be repaired, nor the sense that they had been lied to.

CHAPTER ELEVEN

Lives in Chaos and the Race to Flee – 1942

Soon after the Doolittle raid in April, Ethel's other eye was diagnosed with incipient conjunctivitis. Dr Paravicini, always there during times of crisis, sent her to the best eye specialist he knew, a Dr Nakajima in Yokohama. The Japanese physician treated her with a vitamin therapy, which was really all he could do without more effective medicines that were unobtainable because of the war. Ethel had always had serious qualms about Japanese doctors based on her lack of familiarity with them. There were virtually no foreign practitioners left, however, and Dr Paravicini assured Ethel that Dr Nakajima had an impeccable reputation.

Following one examination well along in the treatment, Dr Nakajima faced the worried couple across his desk and said with delicate firmness that while the vitamin therapy appeared to be working, Mrs Baenninger was facing the risk of total blindness every day she stayed on in Japan, where there were more than thirty different germs that could cause conjunctivitis. With the limited means at his disposal, the doctor could not assure Ethel that he could protect her from them. She would have to find a way to leave Japan.

Easier said than done.

Hans turned to Dr Paravicini for counsel. Over the years, Para had been something of a mentor to his much younger countryman and he and Hans had become ever closer friends, despite the thirty-five or so years' difference in their ages. They sometimes went to the beach together, where they swam and discussed the world's problems at great length. Through his postings as chief delegate of the International Red Cross in Japan and his long years in the Far East, Dr Paravicini had built up a network of connections at high levels, both in diplomatic circles and in the Japanese government. So as soon as he learned from Hans in early 1942 that his respected colleague, Dr Nakajima, had warned that Ethel's vision was threatened if she stayed on in Japan, Dr Paravicini moved into action. He began by contacting the Swiss chargé d'affaires in Tokyo to see what, if anything, could be done. The alarm on Hans's face, usually so calm and jovial, said it all, and he knew that a solution must be found.

With his many years of experience, Dr Paravicini was well aware that one of the important services neutral countries like Switzerland provide in wartime is arranging for exchanges of personnel between the warring nations, not only prisoners of war but also civilians who simply find themselves in the wrong place through no fault of their own. By this time, all Allied civilians in Japan had been interned or evacuated and there would be no further ships to transport civilians. Dr Paravicini knew that a final evacuation ship was being organized for a 30 July departure from Japan, but that passage was strictly reserved for diplomats and their families. Through his contacts, however, he had also learned that the Japanese and British governments had just agreed to exchange British and other Allied internees from Japanese-occupied China for the last Japanese still stranded in Europe in a previously unscheduled swap. It was the ship that would ultimately carry out this exchange that Dr Paravicini began to monitor closely.

As soon as war broke out, Britain's embassy was closed and its entire staff interned on the building's premises. His Majesty's diplomatic interests and representation had initially been entrusted to Argentina, but in 1942 this responsibility was transferred to Switzerland. The United States embassy had also been shut down and Sweden, another neutral country, took over diplomatic responsibilities on behalf of America. It was therefore the Swiss and the Swedes who were mandated to organize and supervise the final repatriation exchanges between Britain and the United States and Japan, which took place during the first eight months of 1942. The Swiss Dr Paravicini was in an ideal position to keep track of developments.

The first departure organized by the Swiss was that of the SS *Tatsuta Maru*, which was to carry all remaining "enemy" diplomats from Japan to Lourenço Marques, in Portuguese East Africa, via Saigon and Singapore, where others would be taken aboard. But the Baenningers were not diplomats, and that was why Dr Paravicini was keeping his eye on the arrangements being made by Switzerland's legations in London and Tokyo to line up a ship to carry British and Allied interned civilians from Shanghai to Lourenço Marques, where they would be exchanged for their Japanese civilian counterparts transported from Britain and Europe. A Japanese ship would almost certainly be chosen for this mission, too, and maybe there was a way to get the Baenningers on it.

After discussing her case in more detail with his Japanese colleague, Dr Paravicini had become convinced that saving Ethel from blindness indeed depended on her escape, which meant her being on the Japanese exchange ship scheduled for departure to Shanghai and then Mozambique in August 1942. It would be her last chance. With the *Tatsuta Maru*, it was one of the last two ships that would be authorized by the imperial Japanese government to evacuate remaining Allied civilians from the Far East.

The older man's calm advice, the stark health warning, and the sudden availability of what might well be a possible last means to escape provided the jolt that Hans and Ethel needed to make a decision about the future. In such fraught circumstances the status quo often seems the easier and more congenial option. The catastrophe surrounding them and their uncertainty about how to react had lulled Hans and Ethel into a dangerous lethargy. The most important decisions are sometimes the hardest ones to make, but time was clearly up for this one and the alarm bells were ringing. The terrifying and intimate menace of a total loss of sight for Ethel succeeded in crystallizing the couple's realization of what they must do in a way that the grave but more impersonal dangers of war had not.

Dr Nakajima wrote a letter on Ethel's behalf to the British authorities involved in the evacuation and so did Dr Paravicini, but Hans had little hope of obtaining accommodation for her and Roni, as Swiss citizens, on the evacuation ship. Although he did not tell Ethel, Hans knew there were tremendous numbers of Allied people applying to board the ship in Shanghai, more than could possibly be accepted. To their joyful amazement, however, the British response was positive. Mrs Baenninger and her little son were accepted as exceptional passengers because of her eye problems and because Ethel had been Canadian and thus a British subject at birth.

As a Swiss, however, Hans was left out. It was felt that foreigners from neutral countries could take care of themselves in Japan, and indeed most of Hans and Ethel's Swiss friends were obliged to stay on in Japan for the duration of the war. It was not pleasant for them, but they were not harmed or especially maltreated. Normal jobs disappeared in wartime, of course, because commercial activity came to a standstill; but there was plenty to do at the Swiss legation as the war inundated the neutral diplomatic representation with all sorts of supplementary tasks. Most of the Swiss ended up working there.

But the Baenninger family, after two years of lurching indecision and erratic, on-and-off separations, now wanted desperately to stay together once and for all, and so more letters were exchanged, pleading to both the Japanese and the British authorities that Mrs Baenninger and her son could not travel alone and should be accompanied by the family head. But there appeared to be little hope and the spectre of enforced separation loomed each day.

Although Hans, as usual, kept his feelings private, he dreaded having his loved ones gone while he lived in the empty house, as he had during much of 1941. Despite his soothing protestations, that year had been hard for him. Ethel kept most of the letters he had written to her then. As a sociable man Hans loved the company of friends, and he had never been very good at being a lonely bachelor. But even more than that he would miss carrying Roni up the stairs to bed each night, singing lullabies to the sleepy child clinging to his back. And Ethel's absence would leave an empty place in his heart. He would miss Ethel and Roni terribly, especially since he would not even be able to write to them or receive letters from them. The only good thing would be knowing that they were safe.

Ethel could only think of the desolation she had felt during the previous year when she was half a world away from Hans, not knowing when she would see him again. And that was before the war had even started. It was too dreadful to contemplate, and although she tried to put on a brave face, she often awoke in the night in tears. She could not imagine sailing off and leaving her husband – Roni's father – in a place where bombs were falling and there was no one to take proper care of him, and when they did not know whether they would ever be united again.

After a long wait – indeed it seemed endless – the news finally came that Hans was also booked on the ship whose planning Dr Paravicini had been following so closely. After preparing them-selves for the worst it was an unbelievable relief, and Roni could sense the weight being lifted from all their shoulders through the jubilation of his parents. Tears of dread turned to tears of joy and suddenly the war seemed almost not to matter anymore. They could stay together, come what may, and the three of them united could face just about anything.

The vessel designated for the exodus was the SS *Kamakura Maru* of the NYK Line. It was projected to leave empty from Kobe on 12 August 1942 and sail to Shanghai, where it would pick up its large cargo of Allied passengers and carry them to Lourenço Marques. The miraculous development of Hans's inclusion in the manifest was thanks once again to string-pulling by Dr Paravicini; for the Swiss legation had decided with his urging to appoint Hans as the deputy Swiss observer for the ship, which in effect meant that he now became automatically part of the ship's passenger list. The *Kamakura Maru* would be accorded diplomatic immunity on the high seas, whatever that meant in wartime. But all three of them were going to be on it, that was the main thing, and Ethel thanked God in her prayers for what she felt must be His intervention.

But where would they go? In a world where everything was shifting perilously every day, they needed a fixed objective. As a final goal, and after much discussion, they settled on Canada, Ethel's home. They had also considered Switzerland. It was closer, but it was in the middle of Europe and surrounded by the armies of Nazi Germany and their Italian Fascist allies, so getting back to Hans's home would have been well nigh impossible, and perhaps dangerous if they did get there, despite Swiss neutrality. Nor had Hans forgotten the abrupt orders to leave the country that he had received in 1939. He could not go home again. Switzerland had very little room for more refugees, even Swiss ones. Canada had plenty of room for those who had once been Canadian and for those they had married – and for many others besides. It was also blessedly out of the reach of the technologies of mid-twentieth-century warfare in Europe; it was a haven of calm.

The next step was to obtain an entry visa to Canada for Hans. The biggest problem to start with was the mechanics of applying for and obtaining the visa. For there was no authorized communication of any kind between enemy nations that were at war like Japan and Canada. Their diplomatic representations had been closed and would remain so until after the war was over. They simply were not talking to each other. So Hans, with an inspiration bred of desperation, sent a cable from Yokohama to his older sister Berti, which was permitted by the Japanese because she was in neutral Switzerland. She lived high above Lake Constance in Walzenhausen, a tiny village surrounded by mountains in the northeastern canton of Appenzell. Elections were still conducted there according to alpine tradition, by means of raised hands in the village square. At that time, and indeed until the 1960s, women were still forbidden to vote at all. From the tranquility of their ancient low-ceilinged wooden chalet, Berti and her husband, Walter, could see Nazi troops on a clear day across the lake in Germany and Austria, the very people threatening to trap her youngest brother on the other side of the globe. Walter was in the border patrol of the fully mobilized Swiss army and had instructions to shoot German soldiers on sight if they wandered onto Swiss territory. After the war Walter never disclosed whether he had ever had occasion to carry out these orders.

In his cable, Hans asked Berti to send a telegram to Ethel's father in Richardson, Saskatchewan, saying: "Possibility of family returning STOP Please obtain Canadian entry for us STOP Cable reply to Berti Bänninger in Walzenhausen Switzerland STOP." The various military censorship offices along its path around the world all let the cable through.

With no mail service between Japan and Canada, Clare Kyle had been without news of his elder daughter and her family for some time. He did his best to conceal his concern from Minnie and they tried not to talk about it. Pearl Harbor was already four or five months behind them, though, and things could only get worse. So the unexpected telegram from Switzerland arrived like a bolt of lightning on the prairies and catapulted Clare into action. Fortunately, he was a man who knew how to get things done and he was thrilled and relieved to have an opportunity to do something concrete on behalf of his daughter and her family. Clare immediately contacted a senator from Saskatchewan in Ottawa, and within a week he was able to send a telegram to Berti, who relayed the message on to Hans and Ethel: "Visa obtained." There was jubilation in both Richardson and Walzenhausen, villages that have surely never exchanged telegrams before or since. Hans and Ethel were enormously relieved to have this obstacle out of the way; they now knew that they had a new "home," a destination they could go to if they could get there.

The remaining weeks before their departure were hectic. Many household things were packed up in large wooden crates and stored in the company's earthquake-proof go-down, or warehouse, in Yokohama. These same items – a talisman from the past – arrived intact at the Baenninger home in the United States twelve years later, having survived the devastation of Yokohama and the turmoil of Japan's defeat.

The Baenningers' stock of canned and powdered food was bequeathed to friends who had no way to escape, Kiku-san and Arai-san among them, and especially to Max Pestalozzi, who was Hans's closest friend and had been best man at their wedding eight years before. Max was to take over the duties of the International Red Cross delegate when Hans left. The remainder of their household effects and furniture was sold to a Japanese storekeeper they knew well, and for whom it was an unexpected windfall. Another Japanese acquaintance, aware that pearls were losing their value since most of the buyers had left Japan or were in concentration camps, offered to sell Hans a small trunkful of first-quality pearls for a fraction of their worth. The deal would have made Hans a great deal of money, but cash was scarce, and there was enough danger ahead without the additional risk of Hans's becoming a pearl smuggler. But it was tempting.

Hans's Japanese employees, in a dramatic demonstration of friendship and appreciation, saved up their ration coupons and put on a farewell party for their departing chief. There was some risk for them in doing this. While Swiss were officially neutral, it was no secret to anyone that their sympathies lay with the Allies and the secret police could make life unpleasant for Japanese who were still consorting with the enemy. But there were no repercussions, and the staff's sorrow and respect were openly expressed. Hans in particular was very moved and reciprocated their feelings.

Ethel and Hans were still in Yokohama on 30 July when the *Tatsuta Maru* sailed with its large complement of diplomats bound for home. Sir Robert Craigie and his unusually named wife, Pleasant, were onboard, as were the Belgian ambassador, the Norwe-

A farewell party for Hans given by his office staff on 29 July 1942 – also his thirty-seventh birthday.

gian and Australian chargés d'affaires, a Greek minister, Mr Politis, a Czechoslovakian minister, Mr Havlicek, etc. There was not much of a send-off except by the Japanese secret police, because all the citizens of the diplomats' various countries had long since left. Owing to the importance of her manifest, the *Tatsuta Maru* was overseen and accompanied by Monsieur Hausherr, representative of the Swiss legation at Tokyo, as well as Baron Hayashi, a highly placed official from the Japanese Foreign Office. From up on the Bluff, Hans and Ethel discreetly watched the *Tatsuta Maru* sail, knowing that in less than two weeks they would be the next – and indeed the last – to leave.

News that Hans and Ethel had been lucky and were leaving Yokohama got around quickly in the thinned-out ranks of the foreign community and many friends came to the train station on 11 August to say goodbye when the Baenninger family set off for Kobe. No one knew whether they would ever see each other again, and some of the goodbyes were wrenching; as Ethel says very simply in her diary, "It was grim saying 'goodbye' to Max." For others less close, it was unsure whether their friendships could someday be rekindled after the war, or whether they would prove to be, in Ethel's phrase, merely "ships that pass in the night."

There were no more British or North Americans outside concentration camps in Japan, but there were friends from many of the other European countries – Belgium, Sweden, Denmark, Holland, etc. – and their fates were still unknown. They all seemed happy for the good fortune of the Baenninger family, even though they themselves had little to look forward to, and it showed a selfless and heartwarming sort of friendship that particularly touched Hans and Ethel. Talking to friends after the war was over, they learned that the Japanese eventually sent all non-Germans to Miyanoshita and Karuizawa, resort towns where the people lived in conditions that were comparable to those in which the Japanese themselves lived (i.e., not exactly luxurious, but adequate – at least until near the end of the war). German civilians were sent to Katembe, where as allies they at first received special treatment. But as the war dragged on their conditions became less special.

The Baenninger family spent all day on the train, travelling to Kobe. Roni spent a lot of time looking out the window, watching the familiar scenery for the last time. The only Japanese in their nearly empty first-class carriage stuck out as an obvious plainclothes detective from the *Kempeitai*, keeping an eye on them and giving them shivers of fear that something might still go wrong. That night was spent at the Tor Hotel in Kobe, where they had their last dinner in Japan with a few Swiss friends who materialized for a farewell. Roni in his pajamas appeared in the hotel dining room during the meal and said that his mosquito net wasn't working and that he was getting bitten.

The hotel staff found some insect spray and took care of the crisis. It provided a welcome distraction from the awareness that tomorrow they were leaving forever the first home they had built together so happily and with so much hope. It was an apprehensive night. Nobody knew what the future might hold, and there could be no turning back.

CHAPTER TWELVE

Escape: To Africa on a Japanese Ship – 1942

The *Kamakura Maru* was waiting at the pier in Kobe the next morning and the Baenningers were assigned a roomy cabin thanks to Hans's position and responsibilities as deputy Swiss observer on the ship. They were obliged by the Japanese customs officials to open all their suitcases and trunks on the pier for inspection before boarding, so it was just as well that Hans had not given in to the temptation to become a pearl smuggler. Hard as it was to be leaving, it was better than the alternative – spending the rest of the war in an enemy country without enough to eat and exposed to the American bombing raids that practically destroyed Yokohama and its surroundings. It was just over eight years since Hans and Ethel had first sailed from Japan on their honeymoon, but time and history had moved on. The friends who had held the colourful paper streamers in that happier era were now mostly gone or interned. They themselves were now parents in their mid-thirties, feeling very lucky to be leaving but careworn, and scared about what lay ahead.

In her diary Ethel wrote: "Eight passengers on that huge ship seemed fantastic, but we thoroughly enjoyed the peace and quiet after the excitement and hubbub of the preceding days." Indeed, until they arrived in Shanghai (at which point half of China seemed intent on climbing aboard), there were only eight fellow travellers, including four Japanese diplomats. One of them, a Mr Sakamoto, was an impressive gentleman who was going to Bern to assume duties as the new Japanese ambassador to Switzerland. On a couple of occasions Mr Sakamoto joined the Baenningers for bridge. He and Hans had several conversations in which the Japanese diplomat candidly expressed his doubts about whether Japan could continue her triumphal progress toward control of Asia. Mr Sakamoto felt that the war's outcome would hinge on the outcome of the siege of Stalingrad, and six months later, following the German collapse at the Russian front, Hans learned that Mr Sakamoto had committed suicide in Bern. When General Voronov took the Nazi general Paulus and his staff prisoner at Stalingrad on 31 January 1943 and the whole German Seventh Army surrendered, it must have seemed like the end of poor Ambassador Sakamoto's world.

There was a beautiful sunset as they left the coast of Japan, their last glimpse of the Land of the Rising Sun, where Roni had been born and where Hans and Ethel had spent most of their adult lives. Still, they were relieved to be leaving. They were more hopeful now about Ethel's vision, almost thankful that her conjunctivitis had helped make possible their escape from Japan in the middle of World War II. Except for what they had left behind in the go-down at the company, they carried with them everything they owned in a few light suitcases and three large steamer trunks covered with steamship line and hotel stickers, and tags from ports around the world. They had been around, separately and together.

The peace and quiet of a large ship with so few passengers after all the stress and sadness of departure was very welcome, but after four days of pleasant, although extremely hot, conditions the clear water of the sea turned muddy, signalling the approach of land before they sighted it. As they reached the mouth of the Yangtze River, the pilot came aboard to steer them upriver to Shanghai, through the shifting sands and soils of the delta. To their astonishment he was a Caucasian, cheerful and florid-faced, with blue eyes and a white mustache, dressed in white and wearing a topi, or pith helmet. He was the very model of a colonial Englishman who had spent his whole life in Asia – as indeed he had. To the captain and crew of the *Kamakura Maru*, needing to rely on an Englishman to pilot Japan's warships, freighters, and passenger ships into this port they had recently conquered was ignominious and insulting. But he was the only one who possessed the knowledge to do the job safely, so they had to swallow their pride and accept the enemy pilot.

Since Hans and Ethel's last visit eight years before on their honeymoon, Shanghai had changed very little, except that it now looked seedy and unkempt and there was very little motor traffic, even on the Bund or near the Cathay Hotel where there used to be so much glamour and bustle. The manager of Hans's company office, Arnold Kobelt, came to greet them at the pier, a welcome and familiar face in the throng of Europeans trying to get out of China aboard their ship. After an excellent lunch together, they waded through the crowd to get a taxi to Kobelt's elegant penthouse apartment, where they were to spend a weekend in perfect weather. Ethel commented in her diary on the happiness of the beautiful Kobelt home, their beautiful baby, and the sadness she felt that so many similarly lovely homes all over the world were being disrupted and made unhappy by "conditions prevailing."

The Baenningers returned to the ship early on Monday morning, 17 August, for the 7:00 A.M. departure. About nine hundred people had tickets to board a ship whose normal capacity was only 450, so it was a chaotic scene. And there were at least nine hundred more still hoping to squeeze on somehow. Everyone realized that this would be the last ship to evacuate civilians and diplomats from the Orient for the duration of the war, and the knowledge pumped added urgency into the surging crowd.

As they boarded the ship again, Hans saw "Nan" Nancollis, an old friend from happier days, heading for the gangway. Hans ran to meet him and Nan was delighted to see a face he knew. Before the war he had been a high-up in the Canadian Pacific office in

Yokohama and had also been made the honorary consul of Greece because of his heritage and his name. Then he was transferred to Manila – luckily, he thought, as he was expecting to be out of harm's way and safer away from the Japanese. But the Philippines turned out to be an even worse place to be: shortly after the war began the Japanese took over the country and Nan was interned there with little hope of leaving. But his Greek ancestry and his consular status saved him, and the Japanese were obliged to repatriate him, as a diplomat, on the *Kamakura Maru*. He was very surprised by it all and Hans was glad for his friend's good fortune. It was good to feel that you were not the only lucky one.

Departure was a slow process, and Ethel had to stay in the cabin to guard some important documents that local Swiss diplomats had given to the Baenningers for safekeeping and transport to – wherever. Final destinations of sensitive documents were often less important than simply keeping them away from the Japanese. As usual with the neutral Swiss, they were saddled with being intermediaries between belligerent parties who no longer had direct diplomatic contact with each other. Once everyone had crammed onboard, the ship finally set sail at about 5:00 P.M. for Singapore, which was to be the only stop on the trip. The same English pilot came onboard to guide them out of Shanghai harbour and through the Yangtze Delta into open sea. But first, the Japanese staff had to have a bit of fun at the expense of their class-conscious European passengers. The captain had put many of the senior diplomats in spartan cabins without portholes in steerage, down near the boiler room. Junior staff and secretaries, on the other hand, were assigned first-class cabins. They were served first-class meals on white tablecloths with fine china and silverware, while those below deck were served communal meals from one pot, with a steel spoon, fork, and bowl that they were expected to wash themselves after each meal. Such treatment greatly offended some of the higher-ranking people and a group of ladies asked for a meeting with the captain. He listened patiently (with Hans as translator) to their tale of woe but said that he could not make any changes on his own in such an important matter. He would have to refer the problem to Tokyo, which could take several weeks. He then added that Tokyo might very well decide to recall the ship in order to make the changes. That was the last anybody heard of complaints.

The first week's journey to Singapore was *extremely* hot. Nobody knew why there was to be a stop in Singapore. The British diplomats and civilians who were stranded there had been taken prisoner immediately after the Japanese victory at Corregidor and remained in the far-from-tender hands of the Japanese until their defeat three years later. As it turned out, the ship first stopped at some distance from Singapore and picked up a Japanese pilot who steered it in through a dense minefield. When it was nearly in the harbour, a small motorboat approached the ship, with just one white man – dressed entirely in black and looking like a priest – standing in the bow. After climbing up a rope ladder he introduced himself as a Mr Hartog of Lever Brothers, a Dutch-American who had been interned in Hong Kong immediately following Pearl Harbor. He was the only civilian in Hong Kong to be exchanged – for a Japanese prisoner – and was brought to Singapore all alone to join the *Kamakura Maru*, his last chance to get out of Asia. He was obviously a very important executive at Lever Brothers, but even so it looked suspicious. Margarine and toilet soap could not possibly be *that* important, and almost surely he was a spy for someone – but whom? Nobody seemed to know anything, except that once they reached Lourenço Marques he was planning to travel to Brazil and from there to Toronto. At least that was what he said.

That night the Japanese provided, with refined irony, a sumptuous banquet for all the Westerners in first class. The more naive amongst the passengers thought it was just an inexplicable expression of goodwill, but the more perceptive realized that the banquet was a cunning way for the Japanese to gloat publicly at their great victory in conquering Singapore so early in the war. It had been one of the bastions of British colonial power in the Far East, and as Ethel commented in her diary, "I fancy the dinner was a bit of a subtle victory celebration on the part of the Japanese."

After taking on fuel to power the overloaded ship on its journey, they left Singapore with their mysterious new passenger and navigated through the Sunda Straits, between Java and Sumatra. That same night they "sneaked across" the equator, as Ethel put it in her diary, for the mood onboard precluded any celebration of the event. But she never forgot the sight of the Southern Cross in the midst of the endless darkness of the tropical ocean.

From there they sailed across the Indian Ocean toward Lourenço Marques in Mozambique, with no sight of land for three weeks. The passengers got to know each other quite well, and many of the people who had come from Shanghai had horrific tales to tell of the treatment the Chinese had received at the hands of the Japanese. There was an awareness of the cruelty of people in combat zones; one could only trust to convention and protocol and hope for the best.

Fortunately, the weather was perfect at first and the ocean was like a mirror. The *Kamakura Maru* was a slow ship anyway, but because they were travelling under a guaranteed safe-conduct agreement, the vessel had to follow a prescribed route and rate of progress, so that submarines and warships on both sides could track where they were. Every day at noon, they were obliged to broadcast their exact position in several languages. On the foredeck, below the bridge, there was a large signboard about ten feet square, covered with red-and-white light bulbs in the shape of the Red Cross and visible at night for miles. On the ship's sides the word DIPLOMATS in oversized letters was illuminated from dusk until dawn. It made quite a sight, astonishing in the empty darkness of a wartime night.

The ship was greatly overloaded with hundreds of extra passengers and their belongings, so some of the fuel tanks had been converted to carry additional fresh drinking water. This imparted to it a strong taste of diesel fuel. Much to their embarrassment, Hans and Ethel, as official representatives of the International

Red Cross, were given special treatment by the Japanese. They often had dry martinis before dinner, excellent wines, and a varied and elegant menu (at least for wartime), with brandy and cigars after dinner for the men. It was important for the Japanese to treat evacuees in civilized ways, with respect, and they expected Hans and Ethel to accept this lavish treatment. So they did. Once in a while some of their friends onboard were allowed to join them and they seemed to understand the situation. Roni, oblivious to the complexity of Japanese manners and international codes of conduct, enjoyed it all immensely – especially the soft drinks and having his own private deck chair with his name on it.

Thérèse deRomer remembers the trip fondly. She was the daughter of the departing Polish ambassador to Japan, who had spent the previous year in Shanghai trying to sort out very difficult refugee problems involving the shifting of responsibility for two million Polish Jews between Japan and China. Thérèse was fourteen at the time and recalls long tropical nights on deck, dancing with crowds of teenagers of all nationalities to the somewhat outdated numbers played by a full Japanese orchestra. Once the nightly festivities were over, she sometimes remained on deck, watching with fascination as the wings of the flying fish iridescently reflected the light cast by the ship's red cross and special lighting.

The *Kamakura Maru* had a tendency to roll with a following wind, but Ethel managed to resist seasickness. Roni was a bit "stomachy" but did not miss any meals. Two children, a brother and sister, were placed at table with Ethel and Roni at his early meal, and they were so trying that Ethel almost wished that Roni *were* seasick; their mother only made matters worse. The food, though not as fresh as at the outset of the voyage, continued to be remarkably good. The rough seas continued and eventually even Ethel felt the occasional twinge. "One night," she recounts in her diary, "we were booked to play bridge with Lady Blackburn and Mr Jack, but begged off, as I couldn't face an evening indoors unless it was in bed." Stress and uncertainty made the nausea worse and

Ethel looked back wistfully to the outset of the voyage when there had been only eight passengers.

Gradually, the seas became calmer again and the weather cooler. On their next to last night aboard, Mr Sakamoto threw a farewell party for a small group of his new friends, including the Baenningers, and Ethel had the honour of being seated on the ambassador's right. "The table in the private dining room was laid for eight, and was it ever a posh dinner – Champagne, caviar and all the trimmings – really quite perfect! And it was such a joy to eat in quiet surroundings for once instead of in the big bustling dining saloon." Ethel retired early, but the men stayed on in Mr Sakamoto's cabin and played poker. Diplomats are hired to be diplomatic, but some of them are capable of encouraging relationships to develop between people of warring nations, reminding all of us that we are linked by our common humanity. This was one of those occasions and Mr Sakamoto had that gift.

Approaching the east coast of Africa, the *Kamakura Maru* sailed close around Madagascar and entered Delagoa Bay. On Saturday morning, 6 September, they awoke early to the fragrantly scented breezes of the tropics. From their porthole they could see lovely ornamental shrubs and trees that lined a coastal boulevard in Lourenço Marques, the capital of Mozambique, nowadays called Maputo. Hans waved gaily to the people riding on a brightly coloured passing bus and they waved back, all smiles. Another ship was moored right up against a downtown plaza. The sun was shining, and they spotted old friends from Yokohama waving to them from the pier. They were surprised to find everyone from the *Tatsuta Maru* also awaiting their arrival, and they walked down the gangway into the arms of their old friends Lila and Monty Ellerton. They were all given landing cards, and were free – free for the first time in many months – to come and go as they pleased. They had made it this far, the first leg of their escape from Japan was complete. They were almost delirious with delight at the tropical paradise in which they now found themselves, a real oasis in the desert of World War II.

It was bliss to get back on land after the long sea voyage, and they unpacked their things in their large room at the sumptuous colonial-era Polana Hotel, situated on the perfect white beach, while Roni excitedly dashed about underfoot. They felt immense relief and gratitude at the chance they had been given to escape. But while the first portion of the long voyage to Canada was complete, the next leg was pretty much up in the air. The Baenningers had no booking and held no tickets to anywhere.

The mysterious Mr Hartog, who had boarded the *Kamakura Maru* in lonely splendour in Singapore, had gotten to know Hans and Ethel during the trip, and he suggested to Hans that they could travel with him on a freighter to Brazil, for which they actually had, by pure serendipity, a visa. The Brazilian consul in Yokohama, a Mr Bopp, whose office had been just above Hans's, had spontaneously issued a visa to Hans when war broke out, saying that it never hurt to have something up your sleeve for emergencies in uncertain times. The Baenningers' current predicament certainly fit that description on both counts, and even though he had never considered going to Brazil until then, it now seemed like a safe and even sensible option, and one that would put them at least in the same hemisphere as Canada. Mr Hartog himself, in fact, was planning to travel on from South America to Toronto and had even talked about the possibility of procuring tickets. The whole idea may have been a bit crazy, but it was better than any other idea they had, and certainly better than spending the war stranded in Lourenço Marques, as they now were, waiting for something else to come along.

Something else did come along, almost immediately. Hans learned that a British passenger liner named the ss *Narkunda* was moored at the same pier, just ahead of the *Kamakura Maru*. She was an older ship of the P & O Line, requisitioned for duty as a troop carrier during the war. Temporarily, however, the *Narkunda* was serving as part of the exchange process. She had arrived from England and the Continent the previous day, also under Swiss supervision, bringing Japanese diplomats and civilians who were being evacuated back to Japan. The two ships were exchanging their human cargoes here. The *Narkunda* would then return to Liverpool to resume carrying troops, and the *Kamakura Maru* would return to Kobe full of Japanese. The Baenningers' ears perked up. They had a number of old friends from Japan now residing in Britain and they would dearly have loved to be aboard the *Narkunda*. But they had no tickets.

That evening they had dinner at the hotel with a group of people that included a Colonel vonSteiger, a Swiss diplomat from Bern who had been the Swiss chief delegate aboard the *Narkunda* on her voyage out from Europe. Ethel found him charming and good fun, and he was clearly quite taken with her. Hans diverted his countryman's attention by engaging him in conversation. As he and Hans chatted, vonSteiger divulged that there were actually two ships going back to Liverpool, and he desperately needed a new Swiss chief delegate for the *Narkunda*. The colonel himself had been directed to assume responsibility for the other ship, ss *El Nil*, which would be carrying many of the diplomats who had arrived from Japan two weeks earlier on the *Tatsuta Maru*, as well as returning Europeans. These were the very people whose departure from Yokohama Hans and Ethel had watched from the Bluff. But the colonel had no Swiss to assure the safe conduct of the second ship, the *Narkunda*, which was to transport the other returning passengers.

In many people's lives, there are a few times when all the stars line up, when everything falls into place, when the Good Lord smiles a radiant smile and the heavenly choirs raise their anthems on high. This was such a time for the Baenningers. It was too good to be true. Ethel literally gasped when she heard, but Hans played it very cool and told vonSteiger as nonchalantly as he could that, by a lucky coincidence, he was available to be the delegate on the *Narkunda* and would be happy to serve his country in exchange for passage to Liverpool. Thanks to Dr Paravicini, Hans could truthfully say that he had experience, from his duty as deputy chief delegate on the *Kamakura Maru*. He was appointed on the spot and vonSteiger cabled Bern and London accordingly. London came back saying that Sir Robert Craigie (who was aboard *El Nil*) "strongly recommended Baenninger's appointment as Delegate on the SS *Narkunda*" (perhaps on the basis of the sailing cup he had awarded him). Ethel sent a telegram to Richardson, Saskatchewan, telling her family that they were safe in a neutral place and would soon be en route to England under a safe-conduct agreement. If the Kyle family had any lingering doubts about whether Hans was the right husband for Ethel, those doubts now vanished. As Ethel recorded in her diary, "These things do happen to some persons, why not to us for once?"

Thanks to Colonel vonSteiger, the family could now move their belongings from the Polana Hotel onto the *Narkunda*, instead of having to seek out long-term lodging at a cheaper hotel in Lourenço Marques. They were assigned a pleasant cabin, but when Hans turned back the sheets on the bed he found a bloodstained mattress, proof of the *Narkunda*'s career as a troopship and a graphic reminder that the world, in 1942, really was at war. With many apologies Captain Parfitt reassigned them to the best cabin on the ship, the spacious No. 331, where everything had been thoroughly tidied up by the time they moved in. That first night, they went ashore for dinner at the Polana Hotel Grill, just the two of them, after Roni had gone to sleep. They were alone and safe for the first time in many, many months. The *Narkunda* became their home in Lourenço Marques for the next week and they went sightseeing to their hearts' content.

Not everyone was so lucky. Ambassador deRomer, for example, stayed on in Lourenço Marques for a short time but was then called by the Polish government-in-exile to take up a post in Moscow – of all places. Despite his wife's protestations, the Polish nobleman felt patriotically obliged to accept and left his wife, three daughters, and their governess to make their own way overland to Johannesburg, while he set off on a dangerous voyage for the frigid reaches of a country whose leader had already murdered hundreds of thousands of civilians. The family was not to be reunited for two years, but they found each other again in London during the final V-2 rocket attacks of the Third Reich.

Mr Sakamoto and the other Japanese diplomats were also less fortunate. They had to leave the ship in Lourenço Marques and make their way to their new European posts from Portuguese East Africa as best they could, without any safe conduct. They must have felt terrible as they watched the *Kamakura Maru* set off for Japan, the homeland that many sensed they would never see again.

His Excellency Mr Sakamoto and Hans had become good friends during their month together onboard ship, and it was distressing to think of him making his way to Bern, in the middle of war-torn Europe, on his own. He was a generous man, willing to open up about his private thoughts even when it was not very wise to do so. Perhaps he was a spy, as many diplomats are during wartime, but he was an ambassador in the very best sense – a distinguished emissary who displayed the best side of his country when it sent him abroad. Hans was genuinely saddened when he heard of his death by suicide in Bern in February 1943.

Lourenço Marques was a lovely town, with lush green lawns and palm trees, white colonial buildings, and shimmering fine-sand beaches. The port commander, a handsome Portuguese gentleman, came onboard to pay Hans a courtesy visit. In fact, everyone was so nice to Hans that the world of diplomatic formality and protocol began to seem like a career option that he should have considered. Cocktails at the Polana Hotel with a congenial international crowd reminded Hans and Ethel of the yacht club in Yokohama before things went sour. The Japanese who had already left on the *Kamakura Maru* had cleaned out all the stores in town and it was clear they were expecting things at home to be even worse than what they had left in Europe.

None of this was evident during the Baenningers' week in Lourenço Marques. Mr Hartog, the black-clad Dutchman from Singapore, had become quite a pal during their voyage, and he threw a party for them one night on the terrace of the Polana Hotel, where there was no shortage of spicy *piri-piri* prawns, suckling pig, and iced *vinho verde*. Ethel and a friend, Harry Angst, were the only nonsmokers at the party, and perhaps it was the thick cigar smoke that almost made Ethel disgrace herself by falling asleep. Mr Hartog made Hans and Ethel promise that they would visit him in Toronto one day. Apparently, Princess Juliana of the Netherlands also visited him from time to time, so Ethel at least knew she would be in good company.

Another night, the couple was invited by a Mr Jack to a local party involving English friends, the New Zealand trade commissioner, and assorted "odd bods." It was a beautiful marine drive to a roadhouse overlooking the sea, where they had cocktails outside, went indoors for steak and eggs and a fine red wine, and then back outdoors again to dance under the stars. They called in at the Casino Costa on the way back to the city, where Ethel enjoyed watching the games of chance, and then at the Penguin Bar. "But it was just a bit too loud," Ethel wrote in her diary, and so they just stayed for a beer and then went home to bed.

Roni was not forgotten during all these festivities. "Wednesday afternoon we went to the zoo," Ethel wrote, "and as it wasn't too hot we quite enjoyed that. Seeing these wild animals right in Africa was something of a thrill. Such a sweet Baby Jumbo and we had nothing for it! The snakes were really active, but everything else looked overfed (except one of the lions when a small lap-dog ventured near the railing in front of the cage)."

By the last morning on the *Kamakura Maru*, Ethel realized as she did the packing that they had been aboard the ship for exactly one month. "A long time, but it certainly had been a comfortable trip for us and we couldn't complain in any way." The cable had just come through from Europe formally confirming Hans as the delegate on the *Narkunda*, and, as Ethel realized, "it certainly solves a difficulty for us; but of course time will tell. We are not in Canada yet even tho' we are certainly a step nearer owing to this appointment."

The *Narkunda* was jammed with returning diplomats and ordinary civilians from all over the Far East who had gathered in Mozambique for this voyage. As before, Hans was in charge of insuring their safe passage to England and making sure that all the warships on both sides knew where they were and what they were up to. It was a serious responsibility, and Hans's awareness of the challenges he had to meet when the ship sailed on 13 September put an abrupt end to a most wonderful week in the tropics. But Captain Parfitt was a big help – a thoroughly competent seafarer, and a charming man – and Hans felt confident that they would manage, together, to bring the ship safely through.

CHAPTER THIRTEEN

To Britain on a British Ship – 1942

"I guess I'll never be there again," wrote Ethel as the *Narkunda* sailed out of Lourenço Marques, and her thoughts now turned to the next stage of the voyage. The *Narkunda* was a much more comfortable ship than the *Kamakura Maru*, "long and not too beamy," as Ethel wrote, taking the sea with a sedate calm that was quite the opposite of the Japanese ship's drunken roll. Captain Parfitt was brave, calm, paternal, and good company for the Baenningers, especially for Roni. Living at sea, far from his own youngsters, Captain Parfitt would have liked his table to be made up of children. That wasn't possible, but Captain Parfitt was always especially nice to the children on board, especially boys like Roni, whose hero-worship showed in his eyes whenever he gazed at the captain up on the bridge.

The captain's table seemed like a safe refuge in a world at war. Ethel had been very nervous about protocol, but because it was wartime it was decided much to her relief that they would not have to dress in formal attire for dinner. But there were elaborate table settings on white linen and glasses that were sparklingly clean. Apart from Hans and Ethel, the group at the table included mostly diplomats – a Mr LeRougetel and his wife (from the Channel Islands), who had been the British consul in Shanghai, Mr Austin, who had been the British consul in Yokohama, and a rather hoity-toity but very amusing lady named Mrs Houston-Boswell. After dinner the first night out, Captain Parfitt invited everyone at his table up to the bridge for brandy and to see the view. Ethel was impressed with the captain's spacious, comfortable quarters, like a good men's club at sea.

The waiter at the Captain's table was heroic, tall and dark and stately like most of the waiters aboard. He was from Goa, a Portuguese colony on the west coast of India, and every evening he would bring Ethel a beautiful orange for Roni. Fresh fruit was something none of them had seen since long before Pearl Harbor. Any oranges that had made it to the shops in Yokohama immediately disappeared from the shelves and were doled out sparingly.

The ship took five days to reach Capetown after leaving Lourenço Marques, first sailing south and then around the Cape of Good Hope before beginning the long trip up the west coast of Africa. Their slow pace was dictated by the need to appear leisurely so that Japanese or German warships would have time to check on whether they were legitimate before firing off their torpedoes. A solitary, plodding, unarmed steamship flying the Union Jack in the Indian Ocean off the coast of Africa was unusual, even insane. But they made it, despite their plodding pace, and entered Capetown harbour on 17 September 1942. The children's time passed agreeably thanks to the British colony in Lourenço Marques, which had presented all sorts of games, puzzles, toys, and candies to the young globetrotters before they left. Mr LeRougetel organized a daily children's hour before lunch and the children's playroom was open every day from 8:00 A.M. to 8:00 P.M., supervised by all the ladies in turn. Ethel was "on duty" every other day from 12:30 to 1:00.

Capetown was still a British colony, so Captain Parfitt provisioned the ship there, where it was safe. Ahead of the *Narkunda* lay the long, dangerous stretch up the west coast of Africa to England. The Baenningers spent an idyllic day in Capetown being looked after by the Swiss consul and his wife, Mr and Mrs Bothner. Kind-hearted local people had arranged for buses and private cars to take the foreign passengers on sightseeing drives and visits to notable local houses. They had also collected lots of warm woollens for those who needed them in southern Africa's late winter. The many passengers from Beijing and Tientsin who had lost their luggage in transit to Shanghai were particularly grateful.

The Baenningers visited glorious beaches whose huge waves were legendary among surfers – the local ones surfing on their bare feet, without boards. The Bothners drove them all around Capetown and its surrounding areas and took them up to the flat top of Table Mountain. They also travelled to a point from which they could view the Atlantic and Indian oceans simultaneously, with only a slight turn of their heads. It was one of those rare days when they could all forget that the world was at war and they enjoyed every minute of it. Roni, dressed for the occasion in a grey flannel suit, was rewarded that evening for his exemplary behaviour with the exotic luxury of a Coca-Cola at the Bothners' sumptuous house. Ethel preferred sherry and Hans a stiff gin. It was a wonderful respite after the cramped quarters of the ship.

Dinner was served in the consul's palatial dining room, where a fire burned in the grate and servants offered the beautiful food and wine. After all they had been through, Ethel felt drugged by the decadence of it all. After dinner they went to the movies and saw *Bittersweet*, and although Roni fell asleep halfway through the show, he awoke in time to join lustily in singing "God Save the King" when the film ended. By the time they all got back to the ship and settled into their cozy cabin for the night, Ethel might just have whispered "yes" had someone suggested they end their trip in Capetown.

The next morning Ethel and Roni went ashore for breakfast at a tearoom called Cleghorn's. It was wonderful to see men and women in British uniform again and not to be afraid of speaking English openly. British money was a different story, and when Ethel was charged half a crown for the taxi back to the ship she was not sure whether it was a bargain or not. Mr Bothner and his wife gave a luncheon at the Waldorf Hotel for the Swiss delegate and Mrs Baenninger, and the American consul and his wife were also in the party.

When they got back to the ship in time for the five o'clock departure, two passengers were missing: a Greek sailor and a Norwegian sailor; but the ship sailed on time anyway. "Mr Delegate," as Ethel teasingly called Hans, could have a clear conscience, because although the international agreement under whose terms they sailed strictly forbade the picking up of any passengers during the voyage, it said nothing about dropping them off. Still, the South African authorities were probably not amused.

The safety of the *Narkunda* and its more than nine hundred passengers hung by a slender thread. A cable guaranteeing their safe passage from Capetown to Liverpool had not arrived. The cable was to be sent from the very heart of Nazi Germany, the Reich's chancellery in Berlin, to the headquarters of the British Admiralty in London, and then relayed to Capetown. Like many other communications between the warring nations it was sent via the Swiss Foreign Office in Bern. In theory, warships of both sides would abide by the order as long as they were certain the *Narkunda* was the right ship.

Any U-boat commander who had the *Narkunda* in the cross hairs of his periscope could not really break radio silence. He could not lose the element of surprise by sending a radio message to Captain Parfitt, asking politely whether his ship was really the one they were not supposed to blow out of the water. Any captain would say that his ship should have a safe passage and would immediately start zigzagging and dropping depth charges. There had to be a way of positively identifying the civilian exchange ship from a distance, and the best way was to follow a prescribed course exactly, staying on a rigid schedule to ensure that they were always in the right, prearranged place at the right time. One of

Hans's jobs as the Swiss government representative was to broad-cast their position regularly, making sure it corresponded to where they were supposed to be.

So their departure at exactly 5:00 P.M. was critical. At 4:45 there was still no cable from Berlin. Captain Parfitt was sitting nervously in his cabin with the British High Commissioner to South Africa and the port commander for Capetown when Hans and the Swiss consul arrived back at the ship after the long lun-cheon party. At five minutes to five the captain said, "Well Mr Baenninger, you are in charge. Are we sailing, or waiting for the cable?" It was an agonizing choice for a Swiss, who can never imagine being late for anything, ever. Without hesitation but with a very dry mouth and a beating heart, Hans replied that the ship would sail at five o'clock sharp. He was sure that the official safe-conduct cable must be on the way, and the *Narkunda* was sailing fully lighted, with a huge red cross painted on the deck for air-planes that might be tempted to bomb such an easy target. If they did not reach where they were supposed to be at noon the next day there was a chance that nine hundred innocent lives would be lost. The prospect snapped Hans and Ethel back from their pleas-ant interlude of sightseeing to a frightening reality.

At 11:00 P.M. there was a hurried knock at the door of their cabin. Ethel opened it to a young sailor who conveyed a request from the captain that Mr Baenninger come up to the bridge. Hans hurried up in pyjamas, a bathrobe, and an overcoat and found Captain Parfitt similarly attired. A confusing cable had just arrived asking for confirmation with Capetown that the ship was indeed sailing under safe conduct, and otherwise to turn back. As it was, they only had verbal assurance from the Admiralty. The ship steamed ahead, but Hans and Captain Parfitt cabled Cape-town for written confirmation. Colonel vonSteiger and Sir Robert Craigie, who were not far behind on *El Nil*, expected regulations to be followed to the letter, and it was better to have something in writing.

The next night, Hans was again aroused and asked to go to the bridge, but this time he found the captain far less tense. The cable from the Admiralty had just arrived, so they would be safe all the way to Liverpool. After cabling *El Nil*, Hans and the captain sat down and had a whisky together, sharing the relief and drinking a toast to the long trip ahead. Hans had another whisky with a frightened Ethel when he got back to their cabin.

The next night at dinner they all laughed about the administrative foul-up and drank to what they hoped would be a truly safe conduct. Parfitt insisted that their port be drunk to the sailor's toast, "Sweethearts and wives, may they never meet." The ladies giggled and substituted "husbands" for "wives" in their version, although Ethel doubted that any of the ladies at the captain's table had a lurid past to conceal. She certainly knew that she didn't.

The next three weeks felt like a vacation cruise, with blue skies and calm seas every day. The children's hour for dining was normally a pretty chaotic time, but Roni was at a table organized by the governess of Sir Andrew and Lady Noble's children, and there were never, or at least seldom, any tantrums. One evening they all attended a concert and a collection was taken in aid of the Seamen's Missions. Attractions during the evening included a clever ventriloquist, a Dutch chorus, songs by a Madame Toussaint (whose stage name was Mary Stewart), and a modern number as well as a portion of a Grieg concerto on the piano played by the purser, who had been with the Vienna Philharmonic before war changed everyone's plans. The grand piano in the salon had seen better days, but it was good enough and the soirée ended up with a rollicking singsong. At such times it was hard to remember that it was late in the summer of 1942 and that they were at sea in a world at war, being watched by submarines and reconnaissance planes from both sides.

Fresh running water was only available for one hour in the morning and another hour in the evening. Ethel made friends with the bath steward, however, and when preparing her bath in the evening he always left a container of hot seawater in the corner, a preferential and normally forbidden luxury that Ethel greatly enjoyed, although she could not really explain it. He seemed very taken with her charm and did not do the same for the "sahib," as he called Hans.

Ethel ducked church on their first Sunday on board, as she feared the service would be too elaborate and high church for her taste. The captain, who conducted the services himself, reproached Ethel that night at dinner for her absence. He assured her that the service was in fact very simple and offered to hold her hand while conducting it if she were nervous. "Mrs Delegate" could not quite imagine the captain behaving in such a way, but she loved the flirtation and admitted in her diary that "strange things happen at sea." No strange things did happen, but she and the captain became fast friends during the voyage. "And this morning the Captain said, 'Good morning Ethel' with practically no quotes. I sat beside him for that." Sixty years ago, the use of first names was by no means usual.

The weather was getting hotter by the day as they steamed north towards the equator, but the sea was ever calmer. "There is so little motion," Ethel wrote, "that at times one almost forgets one is at sea." Ethel felt rotten for a couple of days, and then she got an infected foot. The doctor saw to her, but she still felt "low as a snake." The lack of fresh food and the claustrophobia of shipboard life began to get on her nerves, although she did her best to remain cheerful in front of Roni and Hans. Her diary, however, tells the true story, and even her fast friend the captain could occasionally irritate her. "Sometimes these people depress me horribly. Seating accommodation at table sometimes very difficult. Hans and I arrive first for example, and the Captain changes his place and comes and sits between us. I wish I were clever and could express my thoughts. Simply couldn't face dinner."

Still, Hans and Ethel at least were lucky to have special privileges because of Hans's position. Most couples were separated from each other, the men sleeping in all-male cabins and the women bunked together as well. This made for lots of irritability and frustration as time wore on. The captain also noted a sharp increase in heavy petting sessions going on at night in the darker corners of the upper decks. With a typical male cast on things, he assumed that it was all wonderfully illicit, but Ethel believed it was probably just respectable married couples trying to sneak a moment of privacy together.

Most days there was little motion. On the second Saturday evening, Ethel and Hans were invited to a locker party on c deck by Mr and Mrs Phillips. Both dressed in white sharkskin that night "because Hans decided he should look really respectable for once." The Baenningers must have looked very glamorous that evening, their deep tans contrasting with the pale fabric, Ethel drinking red wine and Hans sipping very strong gin prepared by the purser. They made an attractive couple as they sailed in the tropical twilight, up the west coast of Africa. Ethel's glamour did not go unnoticed, even among the younger passengers. "Had my hand charmingly kissed today by the older of the two young Klass boys. I was really quite enchanted. We were saying goodnight to them and their governess, and Roni was arranging to play with them again tomorrow, and the older boy took my hand so sweetly and kissed it. It was such a charming simple gesture that it made me feel like a queen."

On clear sunny days they could sometimes see land to the east, but they were not permitted to stop. The original plan had called for them to sail first to the Azores, but then the Admiralty cabled to direct them to the Cape Verde Islands instead. There they took on fuel, water, and fresh fruits and vegetables. As a Portuguese colony the islands were neutral, and according to the rulebook only Hans, as delegate and a neutral Swiss, was allowed to go ashore. He spent a very odd day as a reluctant, solitary, and slightly resentful tourist, being shown around the Cape Verde Islands by insistent local officials who spoke only Portuguese. The main crop seemed to be a plant from which castor oil was extracted, and castor oil was the principal export. Hans made a brave show of interest, smiled a lot, and learned a little about topics that were entirely peripheral to his interests. He spoke as much Portuguese as he could remember from when he studied the language in Lourenço Marques. All in all it seemed like a very dreary place and Ethel did not envy Hans his day on dry land.

Back on board the *Narkunda* Ethel and Roni were greatly entertained by the divers in heavily laden rowboats who came alongside selling fresh fruit. Baskets containing oranges, mangos, papayas, and breadfruit were raised up to the ship's rail on ropes. The passengers tossed down their coins, which the sellers usually had to dive for. Roni was fascinated by the soles of the divers' feet and by the palms of their hands. Those parts of them were the same colour as his, although all their other parts were very much darker. To a young boy who had never been to Africa and who had never seen black people, it was a major mystery. Was their blood also darker, and how about their insides? In any case, they were certainly lucky because, the story went (and was commonly believed), the sharks infesting the waters around the ship never attacked people with black skin and the locals were therefore safe, unless the sharks caught sight of the soles of their feet.

The ship lay at anchor in St Vincent harbour for several days. Their only company in the harbour was an Italian ship loaded with barley and corn that had been stranded by the war and anchored there since the conflict started. As Ethel wrote in her diary, "The Italian sailors must be glad to be out of the war even if they are off in a dreary spot such as this."

On 1 October they departed again, heading north, at 12:10 A.M., in strict accordance with Admiralty instructions to leave early Thursday morning. By 2 October the *Narkunda* was far enough north to be considered in the danger zone. The wearing of life vests at all times was now recommended and the atmosphere on board became perceptibly more tense. The seas grew rougher again, too, and Ethel recorded that one night at about 3:00 A.M., after Hans had already had to drown a mouse that had awakened them with its scrabbling in the wash basin, "a plate with four apples in it fell to the floor and I had to get up and chase apples around for awhile – not so quickly gathered in either, in the half light and with the ship rolling from side to side. I really slept very little last night."

While Roni was at the children's hour one morning, Ethel and Hans spent time down in the baggage room, putting all their summer clothing away and taking out the woollens and heavier clothing they would need now that they were leaving the tropics. On 4 October, their fourth Sunday on board, the normal church ceremony was devoted to funeral services for Reverend Father Ward, a frail Roman Catholic priest who had died on Friday night. Fortunately there was another Catholic priest on board who could officiate. The ship's Union Jack flew at half-mast in honour of the deceased and Ethel thought it was one of the most desolating things she had ever seen.

Today Roni has very few memories of shipboard life on either the *Kamakura Maru* or the *Narkunda*. There were lots of other passengers, and the crew were mostly friendly. The smells on board a ship – salt air, fresh paint, the burning coal from huge steam engines, the intoxicating scents of tropical vegetation wafting out to sea from the African coast – these still stir up memories after sixty years. The *Narkunda* stayed well out in the Atlantic as it passed North Africa, Gibraltar, and the Iberian Peninsula, but the ship was close enough to land so that those onboard were able to see houses in the Azores. There were very few other ships to be seen, friendly or unfriendly, alone like the *Narkunda* or in convoys. This was probably just as well, since the lumbering, overloaded *Narkunda* lacked enough lifeboats to accommodate all the passengers aboard. She was fully lit at night so that enemy aircraft would at least pause before they attacked. That was the hope, and it seemed to work.

Excitement on board the *Narkunda* was mounting as the ship got nearer to Europe. Ethel and Hans had heard that accommodations were very hard to find in both Liverpool and London and they hoped that the Swiss legation would not have forgotten them.

It was now only a few days before their arrival. Another chapter in their voyage was coming to an end, and they were not sorry.

"Generally speaking," as Ethel recounts in her diary,

an extraordinary crowd of people on board these ships. We started out expecting a wonderful spirit of co-operation – everybody in the same position and all that sort of thing – each understanding the other's difficulties. But it's simply a case of every man for himself and the devil take the hindmost. All this squabbling over priority has been such a surprise. As for filching of packets with sugar and biscuits from the table, one would say, well it just isn't done. *But it is!* Table steward (Roni's) told us of one man passenger who said he had saved 1 ¼ lbs of sugar from the table in one week and he hoped to have five lbs by the time he reached England. Result, of course, sugar had to be rationed at the table. Mrs LeRougetel remarked the other day that a trip like this would be good for anyone who had an excessive faith in human nature. He or she would be cured completely. And I agree most emphatically. One ceases being surprised at anything. Someone trying to crawl out into the lifeboats and take pictures during Father Ward's funeral the other day was one thing that really shocked me.

But as the end of the voyage grew closer, people who had gotten on their nerves suddenly began to seem much more agreeable and small annoyances in shipboard life that had been really irritating just a week before began to seem funny, things to remember, like a good joke. Especially at such times, one is grateful for the enduring human capacity to let good memories gradually obscure the bad ones.

In the wee hours of Saturday, 10 October 1942, the *Narkunda* arrived at the entrance to the Mersey Canal outside Liverpool. The trip from Capetown had taken just over three weeks, with hostile vessels lurking beneath the surface of the sea for most of the voyage. All the passengers were grateful that they had not had to join them.

The Baenningers had made it through the longest ocean voyage of their lives, healthy, happy, and free of disease. They had not been bombed, torpedoed, or even chased. The idea that someone out there might try to sink the ship, might want to hurt them, never really occurred to Roni. Hans and Ethel thanked their lucky stars that they were all safe again. As so often when they were immensely relieved about something, they burst into song – this time with a chorus of "There'll Always Be an England." Roni hummed along; it seemed to be safe for him to do that now that they actually *were* in England and there were no Japanese soldiers to overhear him.

Ahead in the Mersey River channel lay dozens of freighters and transport ships, part of a large convoy that had just made it across the Atlantic from Canada, carrying goods that helped to sustain Great Britain throughout the war. Behind the *Narkunda*, amazingly, was *El Nil*. They had followed the leader safely all the way from Capetown. Floating in the long queue of ships outside the Liverpool docks suddenly seemed a very small inconvenience. All the waiting civilian passengers tried to imagine the dangers faced by all those grey ships and their heroic crews who had survived the stormy waters of the North Atlantic. But their protection was tangible. Nazi U-boats had been kept at bay by destroyer escorts of the British navy. All that had protected the *Narkunda*, *Kamakura Maru*, and *El Nil* were international safe-conduct agreements, administered by Hans Baenninger. And he didn't even own a gun – although Roni was proud to have his grandfather's old policeman's truncheon.

The next day it would be exactly two months since the Baenningers had left Kobe on their voyage "home" – wherever that was. They began in the Pacific Ocean, traversed the whole breadth of the Indian Ocean, and ended halfway across the world in the North Atlantic. Maybe they had been lucky. Maybe the reconnaissance planes and warships of the US and Britain had simply missed the *Kamakura Maru* as she sailed from Kobe to Lourenço Marques; perhaps the Nazi U-boats had just not spotted the

Narkunda between Lourenço Marques and Liverpool. Cooperative agreements among nations at war with each other seem a weak form of protection, a slender reed on which to place one's hopes for safety and salvation. Yet it seemed that the agreement had held. Hans had never once had to make radio contact with hostile aircraft or ships, had never spoken with a ship's captain who was considering whether to torpedo the *Narkunda*. The bad guys had left them alone because there was an international agreement to do so, as long as the ship followed the rules prescribed and agreed to by the warring nations. The radio signal that Hans broadcast daily at noon during those weeks at sea had been enough to ward off attack. In the craziness of a world at war it seemed incredibly sane that such a small, insignificant act should have been enough to keep more than nine hundred people from harm.

Later the Baenningers heard that a U-boat sank the *Narkunda* on one of her next voyages when she was transporting troops – without a safe conduct. Captain Parfitt went down with her. He was a brave captain who should have lived on in a saner world to take care of his own sons. Ethel was crushed, but Roni was grateful that he had been looked after by him, and Captain Parfitt remained firmly and forever among his heroes.

When your life is in danger other worries are put aside. Now Hans and Ethel had to pay attention to their financial survival. It was not sure who was going to pay hotel bills and train fares. The trip from Japan had been free, thanks to Hans's appointments by the Swiss government and the International Red Cross. But continuing to turn in their expense vouchers for lodging and travel in England did not seem quite right. The passenger exchange was over and everybody was back where they belonged, in England or Japan. Living in hotels as a family is expensive. There is not much you can do for yourself; fixing meals, washing clothes, even making phone calls must be done for you by other people who are paid for their work. The problem was serious, and to make it more pressing the mysterious Colonel vonSteiger had booked them into one of the most expensive hotels in London.

So the Baenningers followed the crowd. They spent their first night on British soil with a generous family in Liverpool, lovely people who regularly opened their home to strangers during the war. After a fine breakfast of oatmeal porridge, bacon, and tea, the three of them boarded a train for London. Late in the afternoon they arrived at Euston Station. Two young women in the dark blue uniforms of the WAAFs – Women's Auxiliary Air Force – asked if they were the Baenningers and then took charge, loading them into a Red Cross station wagon and giving them a whirlwind tour of central London. Eventually they delivered the three Baenningers to the Dorchester Hotel; but when it was learned that the Dorchester was full and that Colonel vonSteiger had changed the booking to the somewhat less pricey Brown's Hotel, the girls delivered them there instead. Like most English folk in 1942, these two young women had not seen any citrus fruit for a couple of years and were touched and grateful for the two still-luscious grapefruit that Ethel gave them. Hans had brought a sack of grapefruit and ten pounds of sugar from Capetown, and these helped to brighten a few lives during the next weeks in wartime England.

Brown's Hotel was managed by a Swiss couple named Walliman, who were happy to have a little Swiss refugee family staying with them. Many evenings after Roni had been put to bed, the Wallimans and Baenningers played Jass, a Swiss card game that is almost unknown in the rest of the world. Brown's was perfectly situated for walking in Green Park and around Piccadilly, and for seeing some of London's sights. Since they had little money, and since there were not many entertaining things to do in wartime anyway, that was just as well.

Next morning the new arrivals awoke to the chilling wail of air-raid sirens, one of the most frightening sounds even when there is no danger of an air raid. Throwing their few belongings together they hurried down to the air-raid shelter in the Underground beneath the hotel. The hotel staff and the other guests thought this single-family air raid drill was pretty funny: nobody else paid much attention to the sirens anymore. London's population had survived the Blitz of 1940, the bombing raids of the Luftwaffe had finally been turned back in the Battle of Britain, and by late 1942 air raids were no longer much of a threat. Hans, Ethel, and Roni sheepishly trotted back up to their room. It was a great relief to the parents, if somewhat disappointing for their son.

Brown's Hotel was where General DeGaulle met with officers of the Free French army-in-exile every morning. The general was very tall and distinguished-looking as he strode to his meetings, surrounded by his staff, all in uniform and wearing those wonderful round French officers' hats. Here were genuine heroes whose pictures were in the newspapers, and they made a big impression on the youngest Baenninger, especially when they saluted his mother one morning.

On Roni's fifth birthday the family went to the London Zoo in Regents Park and spent most of the day admiring the well-cared-for animals. By late 1942 the zoos in most continental European cities were in a sorry state. Outside the United Kingdom zoos and botanical gardens were no longer municipal priorities, thanks to the war, and the animals, like most of the people, were looking gaunt. But the British never wavered in caring for the animals in their zoos and certainly never considered eating them, a measure the French and Germans resorted to late in the war. Even without ration coupons, nobody in Britain begrudged the seals or the penguins their generous rations of the fish caught by fisherman in the North Atlantic at great risk to themselves, fish that might have fed people instead.

Later that day Ethel and Roni went to see Walt Disney's *Bambi*, which had recently opened at the cinema. The thunderous guns of the hunters had a lot of meaning for a wartime audience. Newsreels in movie theatres reported daily on devastating barrages on land, at sea, and in the air, barrages that killed a lot more than deer. Roni remembers crying, but he was surprised to see that his mother's cheeks were also wet when they emerged from the theatre into the early evening blackout of downtown London. He also remembers being surprised and touched when Ethel told him that the author of *Bambi* was a German – one of the enemy.

People in London had grown accustomed to blackouts, as they had to the air-raid sirens, after two years of war. Blackouts had been a part of life in Japan from the time Roni was born in 1937. But London blackouts were eerie. Nobody could see very well, and there were so many thousands of people out in the darkness together. Cars had translucent blue covers on their headlights, and thick fog and coal smog often added to the difficulties. Public places like restaurants had shrouds hanging over their doors so that light from the interior would not spill out into the darkened street when people went in or out. Yet everyone seemed good-humoured and polite and said "Excuse me" when they bumped into one another on the sidewalks. After falling one evening when someone bumped into her, Ethel, with her diminished vision, became nervous about walking after dark. Most people carried their young children if they could. Cars drove very slowly, sometimes with a person walking ahead to guide the way.

They went several times to see the changing of the guard at Buckingham Palace, which was exciting even though the palace guards' uniforms were subdued compared to their peacetime attire. Even the palace looked grim. Barrage balloons intended to slice up German bombers were tethered above it with steel cables. It was a thrill to see the young princesses, Elizabeth, the future queen, and her sister Margaret, waving from the back seat of a big black Daimler. The British throng outside the palace gates always raised a rousing cheer when they spotted their queen, especially when she was with her daughters. The Baenningers also saw King George wave to the cheering crowd from a balcony one morning, and one Sunday they saw the visiting Eleanor Roosevelt being whisked off in a car through the palace gates, on her way to church.

London was drab and grey in the autumn of 1942, but Ethel was amazed to see how elegantly the ladies and gentlemen downtown still looked, very unlike the miserable, suffering British that the Japanese propagandists had described in Yokohama. There were few tourists. Foreigners in London were either military allies or refugees, very happy to be in England rather than wherever they had fled from. There may have been spies among them, but spies tried hard to look like everyone else. Most soldiers, sailors, and air force personnel wore boring, unadorned khaki or grey blue uniforms of whatever nation they represented. In Japan Roni had seen very little variety in uniforms; there were a lot of them, but they were mostly drab khaki. But the dress uniforms seen in some of the fancier places in London were really spectacular, with enough gold braid and battle ribbons to satisfy an impressionable five-year-old boy.

Reg Mocock was in the Royal Air Force, which guaranteed him a place in Roni's small gallery of real heroes. He was a crewmember on a Lancaster that flew bombing missions over Europe. His parents were old friends of Hans and Ethel's from Yokohama, and Reg joined them all for dinner one evening at a crowded restaurant in London. Meeting an actual flier in uniform, a young man only fifteen years older than Roni, was about as exciting as things could get for any boy during wartime. Reg had leave for the weekend, and his parents had invited him to dinner so that they could be with him every waking moment. Flying nighttime bombing runs over Europe was not an ideal way for their son to be spending his youth. Every time they saw him could be the last time.

Inside, in the light, Reg turned out to have a warm and friendly smile, several combat ribbons on his blue uniform, and a willingness to chat with Roni about what he had done to earn them. What did he do in a Lancaster during a bombing run? Were Spitfires really faster than Messerschmidt 109s? Had he ever seen any "gremlins" dancing on the wings – those capricious little guys and girls that everyone blamed for mechanical problems during flights? Reg's eyes sparkled as he described the basic defensive manoeuvres to take when you spotted a "Jerry at four o'clock." He even explained to Roni what "dihedral" meant.

The Mococks lived in Cornwall, on a hill above a beautiful valley near a town called Lustleigh. Their house now seemed empty to them, so they invited the three Baenningers to come down and stay for as long as they wanted to. The thought of a safe refuge in a peaceful and beautiful part of England was very appealing, so Hans and Ethel accepted at once. But first, since it was wartime, they had to present themselves at the police station in Bow Street to obtain a permit to travel by train to Cornwall – train travel was still restricted – and stay on for a visit of indefinite length. Roni went along because nobody could think of anything else to do with him. As foreigners, they were under surveillance and had to be accounted for. The policemen at the station carefully examined the tattered pages and multiple stampings of both well-used Swiss passports – Roni was included in Ethel's – until one of them said, "Cor, Bill, she's British!" Thanks to Ethel's Canadian background everything was suddenly all right, and the family received the necessary clearances at once. In fact, genuine Swiss passports were rare and greatly prized by spies during the war. But the Canadian connection – while Canada was still a member of the British Commonwealth – had proved even more useful.

Before leaving London they also had to present themselves at Canada House, where they put their three names on a list of civilians seeking transportation to Canada. It was a long list, but Hans and Ethel were told simply to be ready to leave when called and that there would be a couple of days' warning so that they could get to whichever port the ship would be leaving from. Advance notice of ship departures was top-secret information in 1942. Ships were often sunk by U-boats that had learned when and where to expect them. The warning "Loose lips sink ships" was deadly serious, and posters in every public place warned about the dangers of unguarded conversation. Keeping information to themselves became a way of life for patriotic British people.

On a beautiful morning in late November, the Baenningers left by train for Torquay, via Exeter, where they changed to a small local train to Newton Abbott. Mr Mocock ("Moke") was waiting on the platform wearing an old houndstooth jacket, corduroy trousers, and a large grin. He ushered his guests into a black Austin 10. It was wonderful to be staying with people who were friends, and Moke must have thought so too because using his car was a rare event. Gasoline for ordinary English motorists was strictly rationed and the majority of them had put their cars up on blocks "for the duration." Once settled in Lustleigh they walked everywhere. The beautiful green fields of Cornwall and the trees changing to their autumn colours were best savoured on foot, and they could catch glimpses of the sea from the high points.

Mrs Moke took the weary threesome in hand. For the first time in months Hans and Ethel could relax in safety with a feeling of being at home. The Mococks had plenty of room in their house, but somehow Roni felt a bit safer sleeping in his parents' room. Moke kept a couple of goats, named Pickles and Peter, who provided the only possible danger in the neighbourhood. They had been known to butt people they didn't like and insisted on chewing guests' clothing while checking their pockets for candy. Surrounded by these kind English-speaking people, Ethel could let down her guard, realizing how tense her life had been for such a long time.

There was a lot of catching up for the families to do after not seeing each other for four eventful years. For the Mococks, it was lovely to have the company of friends from happier times in Japan. It took their minds off the dangers their son faced each night. They used to watch the groups of four or five planes flying over as darkness approached, heading for the Continent. It was rare for all the planes to make it home safely. Parents and loved ones all over England tried to keep up a brave front, knowing how bad the odds were.

Moke was in the Home Guard, like all the older men living in the country. He used to put on his uniform on evenings when they assembled in the village for manoeuvres and marching. Roni found an acorn on one of their walks and planted it in front of the house in a little ceremony, for which Moke wore his Home Guard uniform. Forty years later he reported that it had become a fine strong oak tree that made it through the war. Their son was not as fortunate. Reg was killed in 1943, when his Lancaster was shot down over France.

CHAPTER FOURTEEN

"Home" to Safety: The Last Dash to Canada — 1942

After a blissful three weeks in the English countryside, the family returned to London, where Hans found them all a room at the Imperial Hotel in Russell Square. At thirty-four shillings per night for a large room, it was a lot less than the forty-five shillings they had paid at Brown's. Expense mattered, since money was becoming an issue. Hans managed to locate his company's agent in London, a Mr McDowell, who invited them all to visit him and his wife at their home in the suburbs. There was no silk business to transact any more and the company's offices had been bombed during the Blitz, so Mr McDowell had become an air warden. The McDowells' hospitality was repaid with several pounds of sugar from the bag that Hans had brought from Capetown. None of them had seen so much sugar for years and they immediately called in their neighbours to share the bonanza with them.

One day the Baenningers were invited to the home of Captain Parfitt in Croydon. He was still on leave, before taking the *Narkunda* out to sea again for what turned out to be her last voyage. It was great for Roni to meet one of his heroes again, although he didn't seem quite as heroic in Croydon as he had on the ship. Mrs Parfitt was very nice, too, and Ethel got along with her almost as well as she had with the captain.

Back in London, Hans began in earnest to look for ways to get to Canada. He always seemed to have a magical ability for renewing acquaintances and running across people who could help them. It did not take him long to arrange passage. Mr Nancollis, from Canadian Pacific Steamship Lines in Yokohama, was still very grateful for their companionable help on the *Kamakura Maru* after his escape from Manila, and for the great many martinis they had plied him with before dinners. He and the Swiss ambassador in London, Mr Thurnheer, set things up so the Baenningers could travel to Canada on credit. The bill for the passage eventually found them after the war, delivered to their door in Montreal by a Canadian Pacific agent. They paid the bill, having forgotten all about those ninety pounds that they owed.

But first they had to make it to Canada. As one possible departure neared, the thought of December in the North Atlantic surrounded by icebergs and Nazi U-boats began to seem very scary indeed. There would be no safe-passage agreements this time. Checking in almost daily at Canada House, Hans was told that a ship was expected to leave in the middle of December but there were no details as yet. A few days later, on 17 December, they received a phone call asking them to come immediately to Canada House. The ship would be leaving from Glasgow on 19 December – two days later. Hans and Ethel were given a few small, unobtrusive brown paper stickers for their luggage, with code letters and numbers that would get them all on board.

Not wanting to advertise the ship's departure to every lurking spy in London, Hans and Ethel paid their hotel bill discreetly and furtively, trying to make it look as if they were skipping out without paying at all. They had enough money left to splurge on a taxi to Euston Station, where they boarded the overnight train for Glasgow. It was absolutely full of military personnel destined for places that none of them had ever imagined going to. Most were young, and excited about what lay ahead, so there was very little sleep for anyone as the darkened train thundered north through the blacked-out countryside of wartime England into Scotland. Soldiers, sailors, and airmen were propped up in the aisles and wedged into first- and second-class seating; they even occupied the mail car. A nighttime visit to the WC, or water closet, was an adventure, especially for a still-attractive young woman like Ethel. Roni was recruited to keep her company as she made her way past all the young men, swaying with the motion of the train as they dreamed fitfully of girlfriends they had left behind, or were planning to meet across the Atlantic Ocean.

More old friends from Japan were waiting at the Glasgow railroad station in the pitch black of early morning. Alerted by Ethel, the Hammies (Mr and Mrs Hamilton) welcomed the Baenningers and insisted on having them as houseguests. Fortunately, Hans and Ethel had brought with them all their remaining ration coupons so they could contribute a little windfall to their Scottish hosts. Such things were much appreciated in wartime.

Hammy had worked for Shell Oil in Yokohama and was now in charge of gasoline distribution for Scotland. Wartime gasoline rationing was a serious matter in the United Kingdom because all the petroleum for the war effort – for the fighter planes and bombers and tanks, and the factories that built them, and for all transportation on the domestic front – had to be imported by tanker fleets. Oil had not yet been discovered in the North Sea, and England, Scotland, Ireland, and Wales were at the mercy of U-boats lurking in the shipping lanes. It would have been a simple matter for Hammy to find enough petrol to take them on a sightseeing trip through the Highlands in his little Hillman, but he did not want to betray his trust. Everyone understood and respected him for overcoming the temptation – but the Baenningers did not see much of Scotland.

It was completely dark at 7:00 A.M. when Hammy drove the three voyagers down to the pier, where they got their first look at the SS *Andes*. She had been a brand new passenger liner, ready for her maiden voyage to Argentina, but the war changed all that. Her new furniture, carpets, and mirrors were removed; the salons and lounges were gutted. The *Andes* had been turned into a fast troop carrier, capable of outrunning most of the submarines now waiting for her like predators in the open Atlantic. The ship was jammed. In addition to refugees like the Baenninger family, there were more than four thousand Royal Air Force recruits on board, young men being sent to Canada for training in a safer place.

Goodbyes were hurried and unceremonious. There were quick handshakes and hugs all around, and then the Hammies drove off. In the blackout the passengers needed a bit of help finding the gangplank and had to grope their way up. Hans shared a tiny cabin with three other civilian men, a Mr Fletcher, and the memorably named Messrs Golightly and Lovesick. Ethel and Roni were assigned to a small cabin next door with four other young mothers and their children, and much to Roni's delight he got an upper bunk. The ladder was missing, so he had to scramble up and down, but once he was up it was a private world from which he could peer down on everybody else. Everything inside the *Andes* had been painted battleship grey – walls, ceilings, floors, and passageways – and it all smelled of disinfectant, with a hint of vomit that had not always been carefully cleaned up. The simple military furniture was in short supply, so people either stood or lay in their bunks, except during meals in the mess hall. It was a far cry from earlier voyages. The *Kamakura Maru* and the *Narkunda* had been luxurious by comparison. But the ship was fast, and this was the last leg at sea.

In spite of the tumult of getting everybody aboard, assigning bunks to all 4,500 of them, and making sure they all had eating utensils and a place to stow their gear, everyone was served a generous breakfast of fried eggs, bacon, toast, and tea. Having lived on civilian rations for a few months, the Baenningers realized they were now on the receiving end of British rationing; feeding the military was why civilians were doing without. It certainly helped to make up for any earlier privation. Military personnel stood in long lines outside the mess kitchens at all hours of the day and night, holding their empty metal plates, cups, and cutlery. The lines seemed to fill all the ship's companionways. They never seemed to get shorter regardless of the hour. The cooks must have been busy around the clock. But everybody always had a cheerful word for the civilians and their kids, who did not have to stand in line for meals. They could actually sit down comfortably on chairs.

At daybreak the *Andes* moved out into the harbour and anchored, waiting for her destroyer escort. It was bringing a pilot to steer her out of the inlet and would provide protection until the ship left the River Clyde. After that, the *Andes* would be alone on the open ocean. As the light improved dozens of warships and merchantmen could be seen all around. Most of them were at anchor, awaiting departure orders. Some of the ships as well as a couple of submarines steamed back and forth in their impatience to get underway. It was just about the most thrilling scene that Roni had ever witnessed, and he and the other children were enthralled for most of the day. Their parents were a bit more sombre, as grownups usually are.

Next morning they awoke on the open sea, on a course heading to the north of Iceland. There was nothing on the horizon except the steely grey blue Atlantic waves. It was already colder, and a lot rougher. People were instructed to wear an orange lifejacket at all times, even below decks. One delinquent boy named Stuart, whose mother didn't have much control over him, entertained himself by tossing empty lifejackets overboard and watching as they quickly vanished astern. He was justly reprimanded by a furious senior ship's officer, who threatened to throw him overboard too. It appeared that there were not nearly enough lifejackets for everyone on board. What nobody mentioned was that anyone floating in the water of the North Atlantic in December would have died a painless death from hypothermia in less than five minutes.

The waves reached mountainous size. Some of them appeared to be taller than the ship and passengers and all personnel who were not required on deck had been ordered below. Passengers could still get a few minutes of fresh air each day if they were careful and held onto the guy wires that were strung along the deck for that purpose. Roni had his Dad to hold onto him. This ship would not turn back for anyone who fell overboard. They were moving fast, and the zigzag path would have made retracing much more difficult. And no one could have survived for the time it took to turn around and go back, even if that were possible.

The ship followed a zigzag course, and while zigzagging helped to foil U-boats, it also engendered nearly universal seasickness among the civilians. It also contributed to bruises and things falling out of holding bins, and a lot of tummy misery. Ethel was the only one in the mother-and-children cabin who was not seasick, so she had to take care of everybody else as best she could. Her childhood as a landlubber had not prepared her for this, but she had spent a lot of time on boats during happier times in her life. As the eldest daughter in a farm family she also had plenty of practice in cleaning up messes with a mop. So she was up to the task, though not very happy about it. She began to realize that having servants who waited on her hand and foot was a thing of the past.

Up on deck with the sun shining, it was difficult to imagine what life must have been like for those in submarines, deep under the North Atlantic. One afternoon, because of a radioed warning or perhaps just to lighten the load, there was a depth-charge drill. Depth charges looked like fifty-five-gallon oil drums but were filled with high explosives and detonated at preset depths. The strange devices on deck that nobody had recognized were used to heave several depth charges out into the surrounding ocean. Hans and Roni were allowed to stay on deck during the firing of the charges. The muffled "ha-rump" sounds from deep in the ocean were certainly obvious, and the two excited Baenningers tried as hard as they could to make out debris in the disturbance that arrived at the surface a few seconds later – without success, which was probably just as well. They would both have felt very sorry for those young Germans blown to bits or floating in the ocean. On

ROYAL MAIL LINES

DINNER

Consommé Brunoise

Poached Salmon, Hollandaise

Roast Larded Fillet of Beef

Cauliflower

Baked & Boiled Potatoes

COLD MEATS

York Ham   Ox Tongue

Salad

Coffee Ice Cream

Cheese   Coffee

Thursday, 24th December, 1942.

BREAKFAST TO-MORROW.		
1st SITTING	-	0530.
2nd ,,	-	0615.
3rd ,,	-	0700.

On Christmas Eve of 1942, the Royal Mail Lines' ss *Andes* was still able to supply a menu, even though there were more than 4,000 military personnel and refugees on board en route to Halifax from Glasgow. The *Andes* was sunk by a U-boat on a subsequent voyage.

the following afternoon the ship passed near the southern tip of Greenland and the sun reflected off miles of ice.

On Christmas morning, Roni looked down from his upper bunk and sang "Happy Birthday dear Mummy," which made everyone go very quiet all of a sudden. Ethel, who turned thirty-six on that day, had become, as one young mother put it, something of a "guardian angel" to the others in the cabin. The ocean was calm and the sun was shining as a Canadian coastal patrol plane (a PBY Catalina) flew towards the *Andes* from the coast of Canada, ahead to the west. The pilot waggled its wings in greeting, circled the ship two or three times, and flew back toward Nova Scotia.

Nobody could have asked for a nicer birthday present and Ethel was very happy with it. For the rest of the passengers it was a very pleasing Christmas welcome from Canada. By that evening they could make out the silhouette of Halifax on the horizon. It was the first time that Roni had ever seen a city fully lit up at night. He joined the other people in the cabin as best he could in singing a happy chorus of "Oh, Canada." It was one of those times when relief was almost alive in the air, like static, and when a national anthem really meant something.

The Baenningers' long journey was over and their lives could begin once again, in the New World and in a new home. They were safe at last.

CHAPTER FIFTEEN

Leaving It All Behind: 1942–2006

We are all changed by the experiences of our lives. Looking back more than sixty years later, the world is no longer the way it was at Christmas, 1942, when Hans, Ethel, and Roni Baenninger arrived in Halifax. Nations who were enemies in World War II, whose submarines and concentration camps were so greatly feared, are now close allies. The drive and industrial might of Japan and Germany are now directed to peaceful pursuits like manufacturing automobiles instead of waging war. Germany is now more crowded and fast-paced, but it would still be recognizable to anyone who lived there in the early decades of the twentieth century. Japan has transformed itself from a nation that, when Hans first arrived there in 1927, was barely out of the feudal traditions of the Meiji era. Now the vibrancy and energy of the country are overwhelming to North American visitors. Japan is still foreign, but it is known. In the period before the Second World War it was both foreign and unknown to most people in the West.

Hans and Ethel's parents in Switzerland and Canada never visited them in Japan during the years they lived there. They were not poor, but the idea of going to the other side of the world for a wedding, or to visit a grandson, seems never to have occurred to them. When Japan attacked Pearl Harbor, it was too late.

But in the 1930s an exchange of letters was enough. Ordinary Canadians like the Kyles were fearful of Japan. It was very foreign, very far, and the country was trying to increase its territory through brutal military expansion. They could see newsreels showing Japanese soldiers flooding into China and Mongolia. Ordinary Swiss stayed home as well and were loath to step beyond their borders, finding the world outside their neutral isolation to be *ganz verückt*, totally crazy. Hans and Ethel were truly unusual when they each went to Japan alone. Whatever possessed them to be so unlike their countrymen?

By Christmas 1942 they were very glad to be out of Japan. Halifax was a thriving, busy port whose harbour was clogged with wartime shipping as convoys readied for the dangerous North Atlantic crossing. The train that took the Baenningers west to Montreal was pulled by an enormous steam locomotive, with an engineer who towered above ordinary mortals in his striped cap and overalls. Windsor Station in Montreal was right next to the Windsor Hotel where the family stayed for a couple of days while contacts were renewed, permissions granted, plans settled; and then they finally boarded the dark red Canadian Pacific Railroad train bound for Regina. The carriages were named after places in Canada, like Sault Ste. Marie and Athabasca. The train passed through Ottawa and Sudbury, skirted Lake Superior, as big as an ocean, and a vast forest that kept on going for hours as the long snaking train clickety-clacked past it.

And then the prairies began, sunlight glinting on the white expanse as far as the eye could see, and that particular smell of snow in great open places, a combination of ozone and cold. In Winnipeg, Uncle Harvey joined the three new arrivals for the final leg of the trip. His grey blue RCAF uniform turned him from Ethel's twenty-year-old kid brother into a magnificent soldier in the eyes of his five-year-old nephew, a heroic aviator who was eventually shipped off to Burma as a tail-gunner in a bomber, where he was seriously wounded. He might actually have flown over the HMS *Andes* with the Baenningers on it while on submarine-chasing patrols east of Halifax.

The Baenningers' arrival at the Regina CPR station after almost three days on the train was filled with embraces from relatives and friends with wet cheeks. The *Regina Leader-Post* ran a front-page story about the returning family, as they had in 1934 when Ethel first returned on her honeymoon with her new husband. They looked a bit dazed in the photograph, because they were. Not only had Hans, Ethel, and Roni returned through several different war zones but they had actually been living among "the Japs." To the locals this gave them the quality of heroes, even though they had not done anything very heroic. But everyone wanted to pick up Roni and make sure he was all right. The tired family finally arrived at Grandpa's farm in Richardson in the dark on New Year's Eve. Driving through the twinkling lights of Regina made even the bitter cold of the snow-covered prairie seem inviting. Grandpa's sturdy Buick had a good heater, and it was snug and warm under a Hudson's Bay blanket in the rear seat. Grandpa carried a sleepy Roni up to bed, just under the widow's walk atop the solid house he had built himself in 1915.

Roni was not thrilled with the oatmeal porridge that became his daily breakfast, but brown sugar and fresh milk – treats in most of the world he had arrived from – made it bearable. Everybody went for a walk after breakfast on that first day of 1943 in a glorious world that still smelled of sunlight on fresh snow. No one stayed out very long in the cold but came back gratefully into Grandma's kitchen. Her enormous black iron wood-burning stove warmed most of the house while New Year's Day dinner was being cooked. Everyone had saved up and pooled ration coupons, and the roast beef and Yorkshire pudding were accompanied by pies and even a cake that Muriel, Ethel's younger sister, had made. Grandpa blessed that special dinner with a simple grace.

Sometimes the temperature went as low as forty or fifty degrees below zero. Muriel and Harvey walked backward in front of the not-yet-winterized new arrivals to shield them from the howling wind. But on the Kyle wheat farm, except for feeding the cows and chickens and milking the cows, there was no need to brave the drifts of snow that often rose above Roni's head.

The Baenningers lived on the farm until September. Hans learned how to make himself useful, driving the tractor with its metal lug wheels that pulled the plough and the harrow, and sitting up on the big combine at harvest time. It was all new and exciting. Reliable hired hands were hard to find during the war, so everyone pitched in to help. Canadian wheat farmers took pride in helping to feed the suffering world that the three Baenningers had left behind. In the evenings after supper everyone sat and read peacefully by the light of coal-oil lanterns. Electricity was about to change all that. Grandpa bought a radio, and the family clustered around it when the news came on.

Sometimes after Sunday services at the little Richardson church the family gathered around the piano at home while Ethel played songs that everyone knew – some hymns, but mostly the popular songs she remembered from her girlhood. Music was still home-made in those days when phonograph records were rare. Some of the songs were boisterous versions of church songs, such as, "Adam was the first man that ever was invented. / He was put in a garden where he never was intended. / Along came Eve and they had a great battle. / He chased her up a tree and she threw down an apple. / She threw down two and they each ate one, / And ever since then our troubles have begun."

Out on the prairies the world's troubles and the war seemed very far away. The Baenningers found a basement apartment of their own in the Frontenac Apartments in downtown Regina, just up from the Hotel Saskatchewan. One night Grandpa was driving them back to their new home across the dark prairie. They could see the lights of Regina in the distance, and the three grown-ups began to sing "When the lights come on again, all over the world." Even Roni ended up snuffling in the back seat of the Buick. Living in a place where there were lights on at night helped everyone – but especially Roni – to feel safe.

Roni started first grade at nearby Victoria School, which was torn down many years ago now. Victoria School really was Victorian, or at least Edwardian, as it was built soon after Saskatchewan became a province in 1905, the year Hans was born. Attached to the old yellow-brick building were two external metal fire escapes that were like three-storey silos. They were only supposed to be used for fire drills, but climbing in up on the third floor, kids could slide down a corkscrew tube in the dark and pop out two storeys down on the playground. It was wonderful fun.

Once again his Swiss network came through by helping Hans to find a job with the International Red Cross in Montreal. So he went east for a while, leaving Ethel and Roni on their own once again, but this time safely ensconced on a Canadian farm. Eventually the whole family moved to Montreal in 1944 after D-Day, when the Allies landed in northern France and began the liberation of Europe.

Martin was born the next spring at the Homeopathic Hospital in Montreal. By this time Ethel was thirty-eight, quite old for giving birth in those times. But Dr Mingie was a skilled obstetrician and he delivered a fine, strapping baby weighing nine pounds and ten ounces. He was exactly what his parents needed after their anxieties and adventures, a sign that life could and would go on. They were all very proud of him, even when Ethel dressed him up in silly little bloomers with lacy collars. He cried incessantly for attention until Martin's no-nonsense lady pediatrician, Dr Jesse Boyd Shriver (referred to within the Baenninger family as "Chesty-boy Shriver" in honour of her imposingly feminine physique), sent him unceremoniously back to the hospital. There, in the absence of spoiling parents who were getting a much-needed respite at home, Martin gradually learned that crying wouldn't work.

By VJ Day, when Japan stopped fighting in August 1945, the salary that Hans had been receiving regularly since he had left Japan finally stopped. Charles Rudolf and Co., his employer until August 1942, believed that they should continue to pay him a substantial portion of his salary, in Swiss francs, even though he had nothing to do during the war. As the hostilities expanded, the company's import-export business had contracted, but they believed the turmoil should not alter their duty to faithful employees. The export of raw silk to the rest of the world, where women were desperate for stockings and beautiful silk clothes, was simply no longer possible. Before he left, Hans had gone daily to his office on the Benten-dori in Yokohama and had visited business acquaintances in Tokyo, but there was very little for any of them to do anymore. During the entire shipboard odyssey to Canada from Japan, during the two months in the British Isles, and while the family lived on Grandpa Kyles's farm in Saskatchewan, the company had honoured its commitment.

Employment at the International Red Cross lasted for several months. Ernest Maag, the chief Red Cross representative, was part of the large Swiss network that had helped the Baenningers to leave Japan on the evacuation ships, and helped Hans to find a job. At the right times a Swiss friend of a friend or acquaintance always seemed to show up and save the day for everyone – one of the advantages of being a citizen of a small country with a feeling of connectedness among its citizens.

Astonishingly, and in this case even without Swiss help, Hans had found a little apartment in Montreal in 1944. There were none to be found at the war's end, but Mme. Demers, the French-Canadian landlady at the Richelieu Apartments in Westmount, thought that such a nice young man, working for the International Red Cross, should be put at the top of her waiting list for apartments (which, Ethel later discovered, had 350 names on it). This naive new arrival from across the world had had no idea that there was such a housing shortage, not to mention the shortages of cars, tires, or women's stockings. So the Baenningers traded a basement apartment in the Frontenac in Regina for a dingy view of a fire escape at the Richelieu in Montreal. But they were together and safe, and Hans once again had work and a real salary. Beside all this good fortune, the multitude of cockroaches from the popular restaurant downstairs could be overlooked.

Because of his specialized knowledge of textiles, Hans soon managed to find a job as store manager at Marshall's Silks on St Catherine Street. He was uncomfortable as The Boss, and the cheeky high-spirited salesgirls made his life difficult with their informal North American ways, and by walking home with a lot of the merchandise. Being confrontational was never his style.

Then the Swiss arrived again to save the day. Volkart Brothers, a major Swiss commodities import-export firm, hired Hans to open a Montreal office in 1946. He used to take Roni with him to the office on Saturday mornings and together they walked through the dingy halls of an old building in the warehouse district near the docks, surrounded by bales of cotton, sacks of coffee beans, spices, and exotic condiments from all over the world. It was an exciting place for a father to take his son. Hans seemed to know about all the things in sacks, where they came from and whether they were the best grade or not. He would buy Roni a hot dog for lunch, sometimes with a container of *patates frites* splashed with vinegar, then the two of them would ride home on the streetcar – a respectable businessman in a collar and tie, wearing a homburg, and his seven-year-old son with mustard on his face, taking a break together from a tiny apartment with a new baby in it.

Roni started the second grade at Roslyn School in Westmount in September, glad to escape the pandemonium at home. He gradually learned how to be a Canadian kid, wearing breeches (pronounced "breeks") and a toque (pronounced "tyook"). He was a good pupil, the kind who liked to have more gold stars than anybody else. But like everyone else he could skate. Hans took him to games at the Montreal Forum to see Maurice Richard and the Canadiens, in all their glory, playing the Boston Bruins.

The four Baenningers in Montreal, 1947.

In the summer of 1949 both Hans and Ethel felt a need to get back to their roots, so Hans took Roni with him to Switzerland for a nostalgic visit home while Ethel took Martin with her to Regina. Mother and son spent five days on a CPR train across Canada and back, while Roni and Hans took a Delaware and Hudson train and then sailed from New York to LeHavre on the *Mauretania*, returning on the *Queen Elizabeth* from Cherbourg to New York. On the way back from Switzerland Hans and Roni had their first airplane ride. They took a Trans-Canada Airlines DC-3 from New York's La Guardia to Montreal's Dorval airport, both of them feeling a lot of trepidation about forsaking trains and ships.

Martin did not start school until the family was established in Montclair, New Jersey, where they lived after 1949. Volkart Brothers had transferred Hans to their New York office on Beaver Street, in the financial district. From time to time on Saturday mornings, Martin and Roni both visited the office, where coffee beans and cotton bales still filled halls that were now high in the air in a modern office building, near the future World Trade Center, now gone again. There were brass spittoons for the coffee tasters to spit in after chewing on different kinds of beans. Martin also liked to chew coffee beans on these visits, without spitting, until Ethel realized the cause of his wild behaviour on Saturday afternoons and his inability to sleep on Saturday nights. Hans was an executive again and had a seat on the cotton and produce exchanges, so he was gainfully employed and making use of his talents.

At the end of the school year in 1953 the family packed up yet again and moved to Switzerland, because Hans had been transferred by Volkart Brothers to their head office in Winterthur, a sizeable city near Zurich that was famous for building locomotives. Ocean liners were still crossing the Atlantic in those days, but for the novelty of it – and to save money – the family chose to go on an American freighter, *William Lykes*, belonging to Lykes Lines, out of Mobile, Alabama, a shipping firm that did business with Volkart Brothers. The four voyagers left from Savannah, Georgia, after a series of delays that took a couple of weeks of waiting at the Whitney Hotel, which was graced with a magnificent parrot on a perch in the lobby. After delivering arms to the French army and a layover in exotic Casablanca, the freighter sailed on to Genoa. Roni and Martin were thrilled to visit Christopher Columbus's birthplace, before setting off on the train to their new home in Switzerland.

It turned out to be a strange time. The boys had German (and Swiss-German) to learn and school to attend, while Hans had work to go to. But since the family was living in a *pension* (rooming house) where there was no housework to keep her busy, Ethel was left to occupy herself as best she could, and she had a difficult time. She met with an English conversation circle made up of interesting women who were free every weekday morning, and she shopped for things the family needed. Her wanderlust had left her, though, and she never really went anywhere. There was not much money, since Swiss salaries for middle managers were not very generous. A car was out of the question, as were most of the other consumer goods that the Baenningers had come to expect in the US.

On weekends the family went for long walks in the Bruderhaus Forest around Winterthur, and occasionally they would take the train (third class, with slatted wooden seats) to visit Hans's mother, brother, and sisters in a nearby community. His elder sister Berti still lived up along the German border, in Appenzell, but all the others had residences overlooking the Lake of Zurich.

From being adventurous young people, Hans and Ethel had become timid about their future. They felt stuck, living in a boarding house on a modest salary with their two boys in a country where they could not feel at home. They were unhappy but couldn't get out of the situation. These were the same people who only twenty years earlier had gone halfway around the world, each of them alone, to live a glamorous life in a culture that was totally foreign to them, and then managed to escape from it together in a time of war. It all seemed to have taken something out of them. But they rose to the occasion with one final adventure.

Hans quit his job with Volkart Brothers. He had never done anything like that. People in Switzerland did not leave secure jobs with important companies. But he was almost fifty, his family was unhappy, and the company had not lived up to the many tempting promises it had made. It was time for a change. Cashing in on some old favours, Hans wangled passage for all four back to North America on *Nancy Lykes*, another Lykes Lines freighter. This time the family went from Antwerp in Belgium to New Orleans, and then by train up to New York, managing to keep their feet on land and sea for one last episode of transoceanic travel before the airplane took over.

In the mid-1950s a huge wooden container was delivered to the Baenningers' house on a shady little dead-end street back in Upper Montclair, New Jersey. The box seemed as big as the living room and contained all the household treasures that Ethel and Hans had packed hurriedly into it in Yokohama back in 1942. Spending the war in a go-down beneath Yokohama, another city that American bombing had transformed into a fiery hell, the box appeared unscathed. It smelled of Japan: of tatami, old kimonos, and moist wood – spicy and exotic with a hint of something burnt. There were even a couple of dried Japanese centipedes in it. Opening it was almost more than Ethel could cope with; it was full of mementoes, pictures, and furniture, old friends that she had never expected to see again, from a sparkling youth that was gone forever. These things had surrounded them in an earlier life that had been filled with possibilities they had lost long ago.

That their belongings had made it through the war underneath Hans's office was remarkable. That nobody had tampered with them was astonishing, and a testimony to the honourable people to whom they had been entrusted. The Japanese on the home front had endured a lot as the Allies drew nearer, but nobody had taken out their feelings on the possessions of Westerners. Buried objects, like buried memories, are safer undisturbed.

Hans and Ethel remained in their comfortable home in Montclair for many years. Roni and his wife kept an eye on them as they retired and peacefully aged. Hans's knowledge of Japan and its language and his affection for the Japanese ensured that he stayed in touch with many Japanese visitors to the New York area. Hans and Ethel took occasional trips to Switzerland to visit Martin, who had settled there in the late 1960s after graduating from college in the US. He became a senior executive in one of the largest flavour and fragrance firms, travelling all over the world – on jet planes. Taking early retirement, he returned with his wife to live in Montreal, the city of his birth. In 1985 the elder Baenningers moved to a retirement community in Bucks County, Pennsylvania, so as to be near Roni and his wife, who were then professors of psychology in the Philadelphia area. Ethel died two years later, in August 1987.

Hans passed away peacefully at the same retirement community in November 2006, after *In the Eye of the Wind* was completed. He was able to read the manuscript several times through just before his death and the memories it brought back certainly brightened his final days.

Martin visited Japan on business once in 1976 and elicited only a laugh from Hans and Ethel when he phoned from Tokyo and complained of his twenty-one-hour flight to get there: the same journey had taken Hans forty-two days in 1927. But Hans, Ethel, and Roni never went back, even though Roni's university in Philadelphia also maintains a campus in Tokyo. Professor Baenninger has now retired after many years of university teaching and research that included fieldwork in East Africa, and he is now a visiting professor at the college in Minnesota where his wife is the president.

Roni, the only remaining Baenninger who left on that last ship in 1942, is aware at a distance of how Japan has changed. While he has had opportunities to return and has taken lengthy trips to Switzerland, the British Isles, and several of the other countries that have figured in this narrative, he has little desire to disturb his memories. Roni, like Hans before his death, is not bitter or hurt. Compared to many Canadians, Americans, and Europeans, the Baenningers did not suffer at the hands of the Japanese. Their remembrances are fond ones, like everyone's memories of the places where they were young – and perhaps such things of longing are best left undisturbed.

Suggestions for Further Reading

The following books were all used for source material in writing *In the Eye of the Wind* and are recommended for further information and background about Japan and the period during which the book takes place.

Corbett, P. Scott. 1987. *Quiet Passages: The Exchange of Civilians between the US and Japan during the Second World War.* Kent, OH: Kent State University Press.

Craigie, The Right Honorable Sir Robert. 1945. *Behind the Japanese Mask.* London, UK: Hutchinson and Co.

Grew, The Honorable Joseph C. 1944. *Ten Years in Japan.* New York, NY: Simon and Schuster.

Hill, Max. 1942. *Exchange Ship.* New York, NY: Farrar and Rinehart.

Kline, M.F. 1935–36. *Official Shippers' Guide.* Osaka, Japan: Osaka Shosen Kaisha.

Japan in Pictures. Asahigraph Overseas Edition. 1933. Volume 1, numbers 1–12. Asahi Shimbun-Sha, Japan.

Japan in Pictures. Asahigraph Overseas Edition. 1934. Volume 2, numbers 1–12. Asahi Shimbun-Sha, Japan.

Index